PROOFREADERS' MARKS

Mark	Meaning
⌒	close up space
ℐ	delete
⌒ℐ	delete and close up space
#	separate with a space
∧	insert here what is indicated in the margin
¶	start new paragraph
no ¶	no paragraph; run in with previous paragraph
⊙/	insert period
⋀/	insert comma
;/	insert semicolon
:/	insert colon
$\frac{1}{M}$/	insert em dash
$\frac{1}{M}$/$\frac{1}{M}$	insert pair of em dashes
=/	insert hyphen
∨/	insert apostrophe
cap	use capital letter here
lc	use lowercase letter here
ital	set in italic type
rom	set in roman type
sc	set in small capitals
bf	set in boldface type
tr	transpose letters or words

The Little English Handbook: Choices and Conventions

Third Edition

Edward P. J. Corbett
The Ohio State University

John Wiley & Sons, Inc.
New York • Chichester • Brisbane • Toronto

Library of Congress Cataloging in Publication Data:

Corbett, Edward PJ
  The little English handbook.

  Includes index.
  1. English language—Rhetoric. I. Title.
PE1408.C587   1980   808.042   80-23739
ISBN 0-471-07856-5

Printed in the United States of America

10 9 8 7 6 5 4 3 2 1

This book is dedicated to all my students over the years, whose written prose sometimes mystified me, often enlightened me, and invariably beguiled me. Bless them all.

Preface to Third Edition

It has been quite a struggle for me to keep this handbook little. In letters and in person, many teachers and some students have pleaded with me to "add a section on _____." There have been times when I too would have liked to have available "a section on _____." But on those occasions when I needed the guidance provided by such a section, I have been able to consult one of the comprehensive handbooks. Grateful as I have been for that help given in time of need, I am not yet prepared to sacrifice the succinctness of this handbook in order to gain comprehensiveness.

I have not, however, been totally resistant to additions. In this edition, I have added a section on the proper form of the verb (dealing primarily with the correct tense of the verb), have given a fuller explanation in the Legend section of the difference between phrases and clauses, have expanded the section on the adequate development of the paragraph to include some advice about various ways of developing a paragraph, have included a section on the system of documenting a research pa-

Preface

per prescribed by the American Psychological Association, and have finally yielded to the many requests for a Glossary of Usage. By adhering to the same principle governing my choice of what matters of grammar, style, punctuation, and mechanics to cover, I solved the problem of how to find room for a Glossary of Usage in a little handbook: I would deal only with those matters of usage that in my long years of teaching I found occurring most frequently in student papers.

Some of the additions I made have been balanced by cuts made in other sections of the book. In almost every section of the handbook, there has been some rewriting or rearranging of the material. Those who are familiar with the handbook will readily recognize the changes, but they will not find the changes to be so drastic that the book will now seem strange to them. One pattern that appears quite regularly in this edition is that the faulty examples cited at the beginning of the entry are presented in corrected form at the end of the entry.

The text has undergone subtle changes in response to the suggestions made by users of the book, and I am confident that the changes have enhanced the usefulness of the book. I wish I could feel equally confident about the decisions I made on my own initiative.

Edward P. J. Corbett

Preface to First Edition

This handbook is designed to serve as a guide on basic matters of grammar, style, paragraphing, punctuation, and mechanics for those engaged in writing public prose. By "public prose" is meant that dialect of written English most commonly used in the newspapers, magazines, and books that the majority of educated native speakers read. This ranges in style from the formal to the casual, from the literary to the colloquial. But because public prose seeks to be intelligible to a general audience, it avoids the strictly ingroup vocabulary of various professional, regional, and social groups, and it observes the rules of grammar as taught in the schools.

The use of this term is not intended to disparage the other current dialects, most of which serve well the needs of some of the people all of the time and all of the people some of the time. Obviously, spoken English, with its own wide range of professional, regional, and social dialects, serves the needs of more people more often than written English does. In fact, many people speak more words in a single week than they will write dur-

Preface

ing a lifetime. When linguists say that the spoken language is the primary language, they mean that the spoken comes first in point of time (centuries before the written form developed) and use (in a single lifetime, before the written language is learned). Also, more natives have a command of the spoken language than have a command of both the spoken and the written. However, despite the primacy of the spoken language, there are occasions when many, if not most, native speakers must use the written language in order to record or communicate their thoughts, needs, and feelings. It is for those occasions that this handbook is designed.

When a person wishes to communicate in the written medium, it is natural for him to resort—or wish that he could resort—to a more sophisticated style of language than the one he is accustomed to use in the conduct of his everday affairs. Actually, in his first fumbling efforts at writing, he might succeed better if he used the lexical and syntactical resources acquired from daily practice in the oral medium. But as the written transcription of impromptu talk reveals, the spoken language is often marked by redundancy of language, imprecision of diction, and loose, rambling, dislocated sentence patterns. Words and structures that may have communicated adequately in the oral medium because of the aid furnished by voice and gesture are something less than adequate when inscribed on paper. For effective written communication, words must be more precise, structures tighter, and organization more discernible; and graphic devices of punctuation and mechanics must be relied on to do what the intonation of the voice does in the oral medium. The kind of public prose used by newscasters on television and radio and by writers in newspapers, magazines, and books has proven to be the most efficient medium for communicating on paper with a general audience.

In this little handbook, I concentrate on those matters of grammar, style, paragraphing, punctuation, and mechanics that from years of experience in reading student papers and responding to telephone queries from businessmen and secretaries I know to be the most common and persistent problems in the expressive part of the writing process. For answers to the larger or more subtle problems in writing prose, you will have to consult one of the comprehensive rhetoric handbooks that are readily available. I do not, for instance, provide guidance in all the uses of the comma; some of these are never or seldom a problem for writers. Instead, I deal only with those half-dozen conventions of the comma that are most often ignored or misused and that are most crucial for the preservation of clarity. If you master these six, you can rest assured that there are no really serious mistakes that you can make in the use (or omission) of the comma.

Nor does this handbook carry a section that is a common feature of comprehensive handbooks, a glossary of usage. Although questions of usage—whether to use *contact* as a verb, the conjunction *like* or *as*, the preposition *due to* or *because of*, the construction *different than* or *different from*—are troublesome problems, a glossary of usage has been excluded from this handbook for two reasons: (1) to be really useful, it would have to be at least thirty pages long, which would make this a bigger book than I wanted, and (2) even if I knew more than I do about the current status of certain locutions, I would find it difficult to make pronouncements about questions of usage outside the norm of a context. If the writer has a question about usage, he can consult one of the book-length authorities, such as H. W. Fowler's *A Dictionary of Modern English Usage*, Bergen and Cornelia Evans's *A Dictionary of Contemporary American Usage*, or Wilson Follett's *Modern American Usage.*

The subtitle of this handbook, *Choices and Conventions*, reflects my approach to the matters I deal with. Some of the prin-

Preface

ciples governing the system of writing have been established by convention; others represent a recommendation from a number of available options. Accordingly, in most cases, I have stated the guiding principle in definite, unequivocal terms. It should quickly be added, however, that there are no absolute prescriptions in matters of language. Where choices are available, a selection must be guided by a consideration of the subject matter, occasion, desired effect, and audience. But in my experience, the kind of person who needs the guidance of a handbook like this wants a simple, straightforward answer to his query—e.g. "How do I punctuate this compound sentence?" He does not yet have enough sophistication in the use of the written language to be much helped by the advice, "In most cases, you should separate the two clauses of a compound sentence with a comma, but often when the clauses are short, you can dispense with the comma without any loss of clarity." Such a person is better served if he is told that he should *always* put a comma in front of the coordinating conjunction that joins the two independent clauses of a compound sentence. There is also a practical value attaching to the unequivocal advice: rarely will the writer go wrong if he follows it, but he may expect to go wrong on occasion if he ignores it.

It is assumed that the user of this handbook has acquired at least a basic knowledge of formal grammar and that the grammatical system to which he has most likely been exposed is the "traditional" one. Thus when such terms as *compound sentence, independent clause, participial phrase* are used, the writer will probably be able to recognize the structures to which the terms refer. Also, the diagram of structures that accompanies many of the statements of principle will serve as a visual aid for those whose knowledge of traditional terminology has faded and for those whose training has been predominantly in structural grammar or in transformational-generative grammar.

Preface

Thus, the "picture" of a structure will usually be a sufficient guide for those who are impatient with, or are baffled by, technical terminology. However, to ensure maximum comprehension, I have furnished the book with a glossary of grammatical terms.

About 90 percent of the examples—both those that illustrate the observance of the principle and those that illustrate the violation of it—have been taken directly from student writing. A few examples had to be invented, but even these are typical of sentences that students write. In the case of those examples that illustrate violations of the principle, no ridicule of the writer is intended. I simply want to exhibit from prose written in the 1970s, examples of aberrations from the prevailing conventions. In the explanatory matter that follows the examples, I frequently show why the aberration is a threat to clear communication and how it might be corrected.

By concentrating on matters of grammar, style, paragraphing, punctuation, and mechanics, I do not wish to imply that these are the most important concerns of "good writing." What is most essential for effective communication is the substance, originality, and sophistication of one's thoughts and the ability to organize them in a unified, coherent way. However, sloppy articulation of one's thoughts is often a reflection of sloppy inventional and organizational processes; it is easily demonstrable that careless expression stems ultimately from careless thinking. Observance of the "basics" treated in this handbook will not guarantee that your prose will be interesting or worth reading, but observance of the fundamental conventions of the writing system will at least guarantee that your prose *can* be read. Readable prose is no mean achievement. The next achievement to strive for is to write prose that others will *want* to read.

Edward P. J. Corbett

Acknowledgments

Every textbook designed for the classroom profits from the criticisms and suggestions of experienced, knowledgeable teachers. I profited immensely from the criticisms and suggestions of those who reviewed the manuscript of the first edition: James T. Nardin of Louisiana State University, Gary Tate of Texas Christian University, William F. Irmscher of the University of Washington, James Karabatsos of Creighton University, Marinus Swets of Grand Rapids Junior College, Richard Lloyd-Jones of the University of Iowa, Mina P. Shaughnessy of City College of the City University of New York, Kirby L. Duncan of Stephen F. Austin University, Nancy Dasher of Ohio State University, Betty Renshaw of Prince George's Community College, and Raymond D. Liedlich of Portland Community College. Both the second edition and this edition have profited from the advice of dozens of teachers who buttonholed me at conventions or sent me detailed written critiques. I owe a special debt, however, to the following people who gave me detailed suggestions for improving the book: Peter DeBlois of Syracuse University,

Acknowledgments

Evelyn Claxton of Rend Lake College, George Miller at the University of Delaware, Annette Rottenberg at the University of Massachusetts, W.G. Schermbrucker of Capilano College in North Vancouver, B.C., Maureen Waters Oser of Queens College, Sarah M. Wallace and her colleagues at Volunteer Community College in Tennessee, Peter T. Zoller of Wichita State University, Robert Fox of St. Francis College, James Nardin of Louisiana State University, Nancy Bandez of John Wiley and Sons, and Paul Sorrentino of the Pennsylvania State University.

I also want to acknowledge my great debt to the editorial and production staffs at John Wiley & Sons, Publishers. I refrain from mentioning those people by name because I fear that I would omit the name of somebody who deserved to be mentioned. However, I do wish to extend my appreciation to Suzanne Ingrao, Nancy Massa, Blaise Zito Associates and Pica Graphics, Inc. for their efforts in expediting this book's production schedule. I do want to mention gratefully Thomas O. Gay and Clifford W. Mills, the two editors under whom I have worked at Wiley, and Arthur Vergara, whose meticulous and judicious editing has frequently saved me from making embarrassing gaffes in a book that purports to tell others how to write.

Edward P. J. Corbett

Contents

Contents

Style 40–49

Paragraphing 50–52

Contents

Punctuation 60–71

Mechanics 80–90

Never-Say Neverisms (158)

Contents

Format of Research Paper

Forms for Letters

Contents

Legend

Some of the conventions presented in this handbook, especially those having to do with punctuation, are illustrated with
graphic models using these symbols:

1

= word

A word inside the box designates a particular part of speech,
e.g. noun

2

_____ = phrase

The following abbreviations on the horizontal line designate a
particular kind of phrase, e.g. prep. .

prep. = prepositional phrase (**on the bus**)
part. = participial phrase (**having ridden on the bus**)
ger. = gerund phrase (**riding on the bus** pleased him)
inf. = infinitive phrase (he wanted to **ride on the bus**)

Legend

3

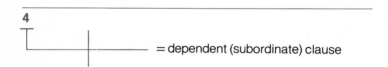

An independent clause, sometimes referred to as a main clause, can stand by itself as a grammatically complete sentence, e.g. **He rode on the bus.**
The vertical line indicates the separation of subject from predicate.

4

= dependent (subordinate) clause

A dependent clause, sometimes referred to as a subordinate clause, cannot stand by itself as a grammatically complete sentence. The following abbreviations printed above the first vertical line designate a particular kind of dependent clause, e.g.

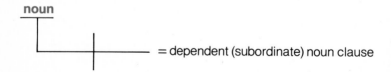

noun= noun clause (He claimed **that he rode on the bus.**)
  adj.= adjective clause (The man **who rode on the bus** was pleased.)
  adv.= adverb clause (He was late **because he rode on the bus**.)

2

If the examples provided above do not give you a clear enough idea of the difference between a *clause* and a *phrase* or between an *independent clause* and a *dependent clause*, perhaps the following fuller explanation will be helpful.

What a clause and a phrase have in common is that they are made up of two or more words. Not every group of two or more words, however, constitutes a phrase or a clause. The group of words must make some sense to native speakers of the language. For instance, the group of words **the big red balloon** qualifies as a phrase because it is a string of two or more words that presents an intelligible thought unit in the English language. The group of words **red the balloon big** does not qualify as a phrase, however, because it does not make sense, does not present a recognizable thought unit in English. Note that all the examples of phrases and clauses are made up of two or more words that make sense—e.g. **on the bus, to ride on the bus, he rode on the bus, because he rode on the bus**.

The difference between a clause and a phrase is that whereas a clause has both a *subject* (usually a noun or pronoun) and a *predicate* (a finite verb—that is, a verb that is fixed, by its form, in regard to person, number, and tense), a phrase lacks a subject and a predicate. In the examples above, the two groups of words **he rode on the bus** and **because he rode on the bus** both qualify as clauses because they have a subject (the pronoun **he**) and a predicate (the finite verb **rode**). The group of words **on the bus**, however, does not qualify as a clause because it lacks both a subject and a predicate. Note that none of the above groups of boldfaced words marked with the abbreviations *prep., part., ger.,* and *inf.* has a subject or a predicate.

In order to consistently write complete sentences and to punctuate them properly, a writer must have a firm understanding of the difference not only between a phrase and a clause but also between an independent clause and a dependent

Legend

clause. Having noted the difference between a clause and a phrase, let us now look at the difference between an independent clause and a dependent clause.

What an independent clause and a dependent clause have in common is that somewhere in the group of words, there is a subject and a predicate (a finite verb). We call the two groups of words **he rode on the bus** and **that he rode on the bus** clauses because in the string of words we can find a word that serves as a subject (**he**) and a word that serves as a predicate (**rode**). We can change the subject or the predicate, but as long as we retain both a subject and a predicate, we still have a clause. The following groups of words all qualify as clauses because they have a subject and a predicate:

> **He rides** on the bus.
> The **man rode** on the bus.
> My **aunt was riding** on the bus.
> **Amy Pearson has ridden** on the bus.
> **Have you** ever **ridden** on a bus?
> **John Morris said** that **he had ridden** on a bus.

Now let us consider the crucial difference between an independent clause and a dependent clause. As its name implies, an independent clause can stand by itself. A dependent clause cannot stand by itself. We can put an independent clause down on paper with an initial capital letter and a period at the end—e.g. **His mother rode on the bus.**—and have a sentence. But simply by adding some subordinating word to the front end of that group of words, we change it from an independent clause to a dependent one—**when his mother rode on the bus.** By adding the subordinating conjunction *when*, we make this group of words *depend* on an independent clause for its completion—e.g. **When his mother rode on the bus, the axle broke.** Adding any subordinating conjunction, (*because, if, although, etc.*) to the front end of a clause or substituting a relative pronoun (*who, which, that*) for the subject word will "cripple" the clause and make it dependent for "support" on an independent (main) clause:

if his mother rode the bus
because his mother rode the bus
after his mother rode the bus
that his mother rode the bus
who rode the bus
which rode the bus

If you read those strings of words aloud, you sense that they are not completed or finished. (You would not drop your voice at the end of the string, as you would in reading this string aloud: **His daring, adventuresome mother intrepidly rode the bus on the narrow mountain roads.**) In writing those strings of words, you would not begin them with a capital letter or terminate them with a period.

For further explanation, consult the following terms in the GLOSSARY OF GRAMMATICAL TERMS at the back of the book: **independent clause, dependent clause, adjective clause, adverb clause, noun clause, complex sentence, compound sentence, gerund, infinitive, participle, verbal, verbal phrase, noun phrase, verb phrase, finite verb, auxiliary verb, predicate verb, relative pronoun, subordinating conjunction.**

Format of Manuscript

In preparing the final draft of a manuscript, follow the specific directions about format given by your instructor or editor. However, if no specific directions are given, you can be confident that the format of your manuscript will be acceptable if you observe the following conventions:

10
Write on one side of the paper only.

11
Double-space the lines of prose, whether you handwrite or typewrite.

A manuscript submitted to an editor for consideration must be typewritten and double-spaced.

12
Preserve a left-hand and a right-hand margin.

On the left-hand side, leave at least a 1½-inch margin. On the right-hand side, try to preserve about a 1-inch margin. If you are handwriting your manuscript on theme paper, the vertical red line will set your left-hand margin. Try to leave an inch of space between the last line and the bottom edge of the page.

13

Put the title of your paper at the top of the first page of your manuscript—even though you may have put the title on a cover sheet.

See **84** for instructions about how to set down the title of your paper.

14

Number all pages, except the first one (which is never numbered), at the top of the page—either in the middle or at the right-hand margin.

Be sure to assemble the pages of your manuscript in the right sequence.

15

Secure your manuscript with a paper clip—*never* with a staple or pin.

Many editors will not even read a manuscript that is stapled together.

16

Use the proper kind of paper.

If you typewrite your manuscript, use white, unlined, opaque paper. If you handwrite your manuscript, use white, lined theme paper. Never submit a formal written assignment on pages torn from a spiral notebook.

Grammar

Grammar may be defined as the study of how a language "works"—a study of how the structural system of a language combines with a vocabulary to convey meaning. When we study a foreign language in school, we must study both **vocabulary** and **grammar,** and until we can put the two together, we cannot translate the language. Sometimes we know the meaning of every word in a foreign-language sentence, and yet we cannot translate the sentence because we cannot figure out its grammar. On the other hand, we sometimes can figure out the grammar of the foreign-language sentence, but because we do not know the meaning of one or more words in the sentence, we still cannot translate the sentence.

If native speakers of English heard or read this sequence of words

> The porturbs in the brigger torms have tanted the makrets' rotment brokly.

they would perceive that the sequence bears a marked resemblance to an English sentence. Although many words in that sequence would be unfamiliar to them, they would detect that the sequence had the structure of the kind of English sentence that

Grammar

makes a statement, and they might further surmise that this kind of statement pattern was one that said that *porturbs* (whoever they are) had done something to *rotment* (whatever that is), or, to put it another way, that *porturbs* was the subject of the sentence, that *have tanted* was the predicate verb, and that *rotment* was the object of that verb, the receiver of the action performed by the doer, *porturbs*. How were they able to make that much "sense" out of that sequence of strange words? They were able to detect that much sense by noting the following structural signals:

☐ **Function words:**

The three occurrences of the article **the,** the preposition **in,** and the auxiliary verb **have.**

☐ **Inflections and affixes:**

The **-s** added to nouns to form the plural, the **-er** added to adjectives to form the comparative degree, the **-ed** added to verbs to form the past tense or the past participle, the **-s'** added to nouns to form the plural possessive case, the affix **-ment** added to certain words to form an abstract noun, and the **-ly** added to adjectives to form adverbs.

☐ **Word order:**

The basic pattern of a statement or declarative sentence in English is S (subject) + V (verb) + C (complement) or NP (noun phrase) + VP (verb phrase). In the sequence, **The porturbs in the brigger torms** appears to be the S or NP part of the sentence and **have tanted the makrets' rotment brokly** the VP part of the sentence (**have tanted** being the V and **the makrets' rotment brokly** being the C).

☐ **Intonation (stress, pitch, and juncture):**

If the sequence were spoken aloud, native speakers would detect that the sequence had the intonational pattern of a declarative sentence in spoken English.

☐ Punctuation and mechanics:

> If the sequence were written out (as it is here), native speakers would observe that it began with a capital letter and ended with a period, two typographical devices that signal a statement in written English.

Native speakers of English would be able to read a relational sense or structural meaning into the string of nonsense words simply by observing the grammatical devices of **inflections, function words, word order,** and **intonation** (if spoken) or **punctuation** (if written). Now, if they had a dictionary that defined such words as **porturb, brig, torm, tant, makret, rotment,** and **brok,** they would be able to translate the full meaning of the sentence. But by observing the structural or grammatical devices alone, native speakers of English could perceive that the sequence of words

> The porturbs in the brigger forms have tanted the makrets' rotment brokly.

exactly matches the structure of an English sentence like this one:

> The citizens in the larger towns have accepted the legislators' commitment enthusiastically.

What they have been concentrating on is the *grammar* of the sentence, and it is in this structural sense that we use the term *grammar* in the section that follows.

Most children master the fundamentals of this grammatical system of English by the time they begin school. They "master" grammar in the sense that they can form original and meaningful English sentences of their own and can understand English sentences uttered by others. They may not "know" grammar in the sense that they can analyze the structure of sentences and label the parts, but they know grammar in the sense that they

Grammar

can *perform appropriately* in the language—that is, that they can utter, and respond to, properly formed sentences.

The grammar of a language is, for the most part, a convention. We form sentences in a certain way because communities of native speakers of the language, over a long period of time, have developed, and tacitly agreed on, certain ways of saying something. The grammar of a language allows some choices but proscribes others. For instance, if you wanted to tell someone that a certain lawyer scolded a certain defendant in a certain manner, English grammar would allow you to choose from these patterns:

The lawyer scolded the defendant vehemently.

The lawyer vehemently scolded the defendant.

Vehemently the lawyer scolded the defendant.

The defendant was vehemently scolded by the lawyer.

English grammar would not allow you to use one of these patterns:

The vehemently lawyer the defendant scolded.

Scolded lawyer the vehemently defendant the.

The defendant scolded the lawyer vehemently.

(*This last sentence is grammatical, but because of the altered word order, it does not say what you wanted it to say. Here the defendant is the doer of the action, and the lawyer is the receiver of the action—the exact opposite of your meaning.*)

The choice of which grammatically acceptable pattern a writer will use is a concern of style, which will be dealt with in the next section.

In this section on grammar, we are dealing with those devices of *inflection*, *function words*, and *word order* that make it possible for written sentences to convey to readers, clearly and unmistakably, a writer's intended meaning. We are not concerned here with *intonation*, because this handbook deals only with the written language. In a later section, we shall consider the fourth grammatical device of written English, *punctuation*.

20

Use an apostrophe for the possessive case of the noun.

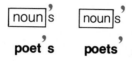

Here are some guidelines on forming the possessive case of the English noun:

(a)   As the diagrams above indicate, most English nouns form the possessive case with **'s** (singular) or **s'** (plural). An alternative form of the possessive case consists of an **of** phrase: **the commands of the general** (instead of **the general's commands**).

(b)   Nouns that form their plural in ways other than by adding an **s** form their possessive in the plural by adding **'s** to the plural of the noun: **woman's/women's, man's/men's, child's/children's, ox's/oxen's, deer's/deer's, mouse's/mice's**.

(c)   Some writers simply add an apostrophe to form the possessive case of nouns ending in **s**:

the goddess' fame

the alumnus' contribution

Grammar

Keats' odes

Dickens' novels

However, other writers add the usual **'s** to form the possessive case of such nouns: **goddess's, alumnus's** (plural **alumni's**), **Keats's, Dickens's.** Take your choice, but be consistent.

(d) The rules for forming the possessive case of pairs of nouns are as follows: (1) in the case of *joint* possession, add **'s** only to the second member of the pair: **John and Mary's mother, the brother and sister's car,** and (2) in the case of *individual* possession, add **'s** to each member of the pair: **the boy's and girl's bedrooms, John's and Mary's tennis rackets, the men's and women's locker rooms.**

(e) Form the possessive case of group nouns or compound nouns by adding **'s** to the end of the unit: **commander in chief's, someone else's, president-elect's, editor in chief's, son-in-law's.** In the case of those compounds that form their plural by adding **s** to the first word, form the plural possessive case by adding **'s** to the end of the unit: **editors in chief's, sons-in-law's.**

(f) Normally the **'s** or **s'** is reserved for the possessive case of nouns naming animate creatures (human beings and animals). The **of** phrase is commonly used for the possessive case of inanimate nouns: not **the house's roof** but **the roof of the house.** Usage, however, now sanctions the use of **'s** with some inanimate nouns: **a day's wages, a week's work, the year's death toll, the school's policies, the car's performance, the radio's tone.**

21

**Its is the possessive case of the pronoun it;
it's is the contraction of it is or it has.**

More mistakes have been made with the pronoun **it** than with
any other single word in the English language. The mistakes result from confusion about the two **s** forms of this pronoun. **It's**
is often used where **its** is the correct form (**The dog broke it's
leg** instead of the correct form, **The dog broke its leg**), and **its**
is often used where **it's** is the correct form (**Its a shame that
the girl broke her leg** instead of the correct form, **It's a
shame that the girl broke her leg**).

Those who use **it's** for the possessive case of **it** are probably
influenced by the **'s** that is used to form the possessive case of
the singular noun (**man's hat**). They might be helped to avoid
this mistake if they were reminded that *none of the personal
pronouns uses 's to form its possessive case*: **I/my, you/your,
he/his, she/her, it/its, we/our, they/their**. So they should write,
The company lost its lease.

Writers might also be helped to avoid this mistake if they
would remember that the apostrophe has another function in
written English: to indicate the omission of one or more letters
in an English word, as in contractions (**I'll, don't, she'd**). The
apostrophe in the word **it's** signals the contraction of the expression **it is** or **it has**. So they should write, **It's the first loss
that the company has suffered** or **It's come to my attention
that you are frequently late**.

Don't let this little word defeat you. Get **it** right, once and
for all.

22

The predicate verb should agree in number with its subject.

1

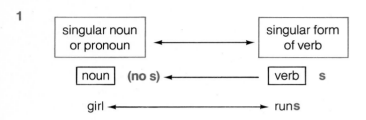

2

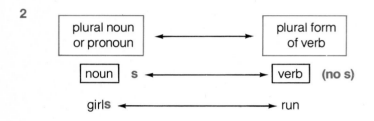

Some typical examples of faulty agreement:

1 He **don't care** about anything.

2 The lawyer and his/her client **agrees** on a fee.

3 If any one of the substations **are knocked** out, we can resort to re-serve stations.

4 The jury **has made** up their minds.

5 He finds it impossible to live with the ignorance, injustice, poverty, and prejudice that **surrounds** him.

6 Neither the gambler nor Jake **are** really bitter about his bad luck or **blame** anyone for his misfortunes.

In addition to such differentiated forms of the verb in the third person, present tense as **run** and **runs,** we have to be concerned about the few differentiated forms of the verb **to be (am/is/are; was/were)** and of auxiliary verbs **(has/have; does/do).**

The English verb has been evolving toward a single form for the singular and plural of all three persons (first, second, third)—as witness the **-ed** ending added to the verb in all three persons, singular and plural, of the past tense—and we may yet live to see the day when a totally simplified form of the English verb is achieved. Meanwhile, the few remaining differentiated forms of the verb will probably continue to give writers some trouble.

Expressions like **He don't care about anything** are not so much "mistakes" in agreement as carry-overs from the dialect that people speak, quite acceptably, in their own communities. Such people should be made aware of the standard form of the verb in written prose: **He doesn't care about anything** (a singular verb with a singular subject).

Most errors of agreement in written prose are the result of carelessness, inadvertence, or uncertainty. The writer often knows better but merely slips up. Errors in agreement often occur when several words intervene between the simple subject of the sentence and the predicate verb, as in sentence **3: If any one of the substations are knocked out**. . . . The simple subject of the **if** clause here is **one,** but because the plural noun **substations** (the object of the preposition **of**) intervened between that singular subject and the verb, the writer was influenced to use the plural form of the verb **(are knocked out)** instead of the correct singular form **(is knocked out).** Careful proofreading will often catch such inadvertent errors of agreement.

Errors due to uncertainty are another matter. Uncertainty

Grammar

about whether the verb should be singular or plural arises in cases where (1) the subject is compound, (2) the subject is a collective noun, (3) the subject of the sentence follows the structure **there is/there are**, and (4) the subject takes the form of structures like **one of those who** and **this man as well as.** Here are some guidelines for these puzzling cases:

(a) Compound subject

    (1) Singular subjects joined by **and** usually take a plural verb.

        John and his sister **were questioned** by the police.

    (2) Singular subjects joined by **or** or by the correlative conjunctions **either** . . . **or, neither** . . . **nor** take a singular verb.

        John or his sister **runs** the store during the week.

        Neither the gambler nor Jake **is** really bitter about his bad luck or **blames** anyone for his misfortunes.

    (3) When both subjects are plural, the verb is plural.

        The detectives and the insurance agents **have expressed** their belief in the innocence of the brother and sister.

        Neither the detectives nor the insurance agents **have expressed** any doubts about the innocence of the brother and sister.

    (4) When one subject is singular and the other subject is plural and the subjects are joined by **or** or by the correlative conjunctions **either . . . or, neither . . . nor,** the verb agrees in number with the closest subject.

        Either John or his parents **have agreed** to cooperate with the police.

        Neither the brothers nor the sister **appears** to be cooperative.

However, plural or singular subjects joined by the correlative conjunctions **both** . . . **and** or **not only** . . . **but (also)** take a plural verb.

> Both John and his sister **have agreed** to cooperate with the police.

> Not only the brother but also the sister **appear** to be cooperative.

(b) Collective noun as subject

(1) If the collective noun is considered as a **group,** the verb is singular.

> The jury **has made up** its mind.

> The committee **was elected** unanimously.

> The number of students who failed **has increased** by 50 percent.

(2) If the collective noun is considered as **individuals,** each acting on his or her own, the verb is plural.

> The jury **have made up** their minds.

> The committee **wish** to offer their congratulations to the new chairperson.

> A number of students **have asked** the dean for an extension.

(c) The structure **there is/are, there was/were**

(1) If the delayed or real subject following **there** is singular, the verb is singular.

> There **is** a remarkable consensus among the committee members.

(2) If the delayed or real subject following **there** is plural, the verb is plural.

> There **were** ten dissenting votes from the stockholders.

(d) Special structures

(1) In the structure **one of the** [plural noun] **who,** the predicate verb of the **who** clause is plural, because the

Grammar

antecedent of the subject **who** is the plural noun rather than the singular **one.**

> Matilda is one of the women who **refuse** to accept the ruling.
>
> *(here the antecedent of **who** is the plural noun **women**)*

(2) Exception: if **the only** precedes **one of the** [plural noun] **who,** the predicate verb of the **who** clause is singular, because the subject **who** in that case refers to the singular **one** rather than to the plural object of the preposition **of.**

> Matilda is the only one of the women who **refuses** to accept the ruling.

(3) A singular subject followed by structures like **as well as, in addition to, together with** takes a singular verb.

(A plural subject, of course, followed by any of these structures, would take a plural verb. See the third example below.)

> The sergeant as well as his superior officers **praises** his platoon.
>
> Linda Myers along with her roommate **has denied** the charges.
>
> The students together with their counselor **deny** that there has been any distribution of drugs in the dorms.

(4) Nouns that do not end in *s* but that are plural in meaning take a plural verb.

> The bacteria **require** constant attention.
>
> These data **are** consistent with the judge's findings.
>
> The deer **are running** loose in the state park.

(5) Nouns that end in *s* but that are singular in meaning take a singular verb.

> My grandmother's scissors **was** very dull.

Ten dollars **is** a fair price for the coat.

Two weeks **seems** a long time when you are waiting for someone you love.

(6) Noun clauses serving as the subject of the sentence always take a singular verb.

That Sara decided to go to college **pleases** me very much.

What caused the accident **was** two stones in the road.

(7) In inverted structures, where the subject follows the verb, a singular subject takes a singular verb, and a plural subject takes a plural verb.

At each checkpoint **stands** a heavily armed soldier.

Happy **were** they to see us arrive.

Among the crew **were** Carson, Barton, and Farmon.

Here are the corrected versions of all the sample sentences:

1 He **doesn't care** about anything.

2 The lawyer and her client **agree** on a fee.

3 If any one of the substations **is knocked** out, we can resort to reserve stations.

4 The jury **have made** up their minds.

5 He finds it impossible to live with the ignorance, injustice, poverty, and prejudice that **surround** him.

6 Neither the gambler nor Jake **is** really bitter about his bad luck or **blames** anyone for his misfortunes.

23

A pronoun must agree in person, number, and gender with its antecedent noun.

Examples of faulty agreement between a pronoun and its antecedent:

1 A **family** cannot go camping these days without a truckload of gadgets to make **your** campsite look just like home.

2 The woman threw some floatable **items** overboard for the sailor, even though she knew that **it** would probably not save him.

3 The **university** did not live up to **his** promise to the students.

4 The **student** should bring **his** schedule cards to the bursar's office.

Pronouns, which are substitutes for nouns, share the following features with nouns: **number** (singular or plural) and **gender** (masculine or feminine or neuter). What nouns and pronouns do not share in common is the full range of **person.** All nouns are **third person** exclusively; but some pronouns are **first person (I, we),** some are **second person (you),** and some are **third person (he, she, it, they, one, some, none, all, everybody).**

A firm grammatical principle is that a pronoun must correspond with whatever features of person, number, and gender it has in common with its antecedent noun. A second-person pronoun should not be linked with a third-person noun (see sentence **1**). A singular pronoun should not be linked with a plural noun (see sentence **2**). A masculine pronoun should not be linked with a neuter noun (see sentence **3**).

Sentence **4** is not so much an instance of faulty agreement as it is an instance of *inappropriate* agreement. The problem in that example stems from the fact that the English language has no convenient pronoun for indicating masculine-*or*-feminine gender. It has been a common practice in the past to use the generic he **(him, his)** to refer to nouns of common gender like ***student, teacher, writer, candidate, driver.*** In recent years, however, the use of generic ***he*** and its derivative forms **(his, him)** to refer to singular nouns that could be either masculine or feminine has been considered an example of the sexist bias of the English language. Many writers today are making a genuine effort to avoid offending readers with any kind of sexist language.

How does one deal with the agreement problem exhibited in sentence **4**? One way is to resort to the use of an admittedly awkward pronoun form like **his or her, his/her,** or **his (her),** as in the following sentence: "The **student** should bring **his or her** schedule cards to the bursar's office." Another way is to use a plural noun wherever possible: "**Students** should bring **their** schedule cards to the bursar's office." In some cases, it is possible to reword the sentence so that no pronoun has to be used, as in this revision: "The **student** should bring all schedule cards to the bursar's office."

Mismatchings of nouns and pronouns in person and gender are not very common in written prose. Most mismatchings of nouns and pronouns involve number—a singular pronoun referring to a plural noun (**items. . . it,** as in sentence **2**) or a plural pronoun referring to a singular noun (**student . . . their**). Another agreement problem derives from the ambiguity of number of such pronouns as **everyone, everybody, all, none, some, each.** Although there are exceptions, the following guidelines are generally reliable:

(a) **Everyone, everybody, anybody, anyone** invariably takes singular verbs and, in formal usage at least, should be referred to by a singular pronoun.

Grammar

Everyone brings **his or her** schedule cards to the bursar's office.

Anybody who wants to run in the race has to pay **her** entry fee by Friday.

(b)   **All** and **some** are singular or plural according to the context. If the **of** phrase following the pronoun specifies a *mass* or a *bulk* of something, the pronoun is singular. If the **of** phrase specifies a *number* of things or persons, the pronoun is plural.

Some of the fabric lost **its** coloring.

All of the sugar was spoiled by **its** own chemical imbalance.

Some of the students complained about **their** dormitory rooms.

All of the women registered **their** protests at City Hall.

(c)   **None** is singular or plural according to the context. (The distinction in particular cases is sometimes so subtle that a writer could justify either a singular or a plural pronoun.)

None of the young men **was** willing to turn in **his** driver's license. (*but* **were ... their** *could also be justified in this case*)

None of the young men in the hall **were** as tall as **their** fathers. (*here it would be harder to justify the singular forms* **was. . . his**)

(d)   **Each** is almost invariably singular.

Each of them declared **her** allegiance to democracy.

(e)   For guidelines about the **number** of collective nouns, see **(b)** in the previous section **(22)** .

Here are corrected versions of the sample sentences:

1   A family cannot go camping these days without a truckload of gadgets to make **their** [or **its**] campsite look just like home.
2   The woman threw some floatable items overboard for the sailor, even though she knew that **they** would probably not save him.
3   The university did not live up to **its** promise to the students.
4   Students should bring **their** schedule cards to the bursar's office.

If you match up your pronouns in person, number, and gender with their antecedent nouns, you will make it easier for your reader to figure out what the pronouns refer to.

24

A pronoun should have a clear antecedent.

?. . . . | pronoun |

Examples of no antecedent or an unclear antecedent for the pronoun:

1 Mayor Worthington, acting on the advice of her physician, resigned her office, and the city council, responding to a mandate from the voters, was swift to accept **it**.

 (what did the council accept?)

2 John told his father that **his** car wouldn't start.

 (whose car? the father's or John's?)

3 I decided to break the engagement with my girlfriend, **which** distressed my parents very much.

 (just what was it that distressed your parents?)

4 The league's first major step was to sponsor a cleanup day, but **it** could not enlist enough volunteers.

 (a pronoun should not refer to a noun functioning as a possessive or as a modifier—here **league's**)

5 I enjoyed the sun and the sand and the surf, and **this** revealed to me that I really prefer a vacation at the beach.

 (what does **this** refer to?)

Careless handling of the pronoun often blocks communication between writer and reader. The writer always knows what he or she meant the pronoun to stand for, but if there is no antecedent (a noun in the previous group of words to which the pronoun

Grammar

can refer) or if it is difficult to find the antecedent (the noun) to which the pronoun refers, the reader will not know—and will have to guess—what the pronoun stands for.

A good piece of advice for apprentice writers is that whenever they use a pronoun, they should check to see whether there is a noun in the previous group of words that they could put in the place of the pronoun. Let's apply this test to sentence **1**. There are three neuter, singular nouns to which the final pronoun **it** could refer: **advice, office, mandate.** But when we put each of these nouns, successively, in the place of the **it**, we see that none of them names what the council accepted. If we pondered the sentence long enough, we might eventually figure out that what the council accepted was the mayor's *resignation*. But since the noun *resignation* appears nowhere in the sentence, the writer must use the noun phrase **his resignation** instead of the pronoun **it.**

Sentence **2** is an example of an unclear antecedent. The pronoun reference is unclear because the pronoun **his** is ambiguous—that is, there are two nouns to which the masculine, singular pronoun **his** could refer: **John** and **father**. So we cannot tell whether it was the father's car or John's car that wouldn't start. If the context in which that sentence occurred did not help us determine whose car was being referred to, the writer could avoid the ambiguity by turning the sentence into a direct quotation: either **John told his father, "Your car won't start"** or **John told his father, "My car won't start."**

The use of the pronoun **this** or **that** to refer to a whole idea in a previous clause or sentence has long been a common practice in spoken English, and it is now becoming common in written English as well. Although the practice is gaining the approval of usage, writers should be aware that by using the demonstrative pronoun **this** or **that** to refer to a whole idea in the previous clause or sentence, they run the risk that the reference of the pronoun will be vague or ambiguous for their readers. If they do not want to run that risk, they can use **this** or **that** (or the corresponding plural, **these** or **those**) as an adjective instead of as a pronoun. The adjective would go before some noun summing up what **this** or **that** stands for. The writer of sentence **5** could avoid the vague pronoun reference by phrasing the sentence in this fashion: "I enjoyed the sun and the sand and the surf, and **this experience** revealed to me that I really prefer a vacation at the beach."

The use of the relative pronoun **which** or **that** to refer to a whole idea in the main clause rather than to a specific noun in that clause is also becoming more common. But there is a risk in this use similar to the one that attends the use of **this** or **that** to refer to a whole idea. The writer who worries about whether the reader will be even momentarily baffled by the **which** in a sentence like **3** will supply a summary noun to serve as the antecedent for that relative pronoun: "I decided to break the engagement with my girlfriend, a **decision which** distressed my parents very much."

The problem with the pronoun reference in sentence **4** stems from the linguistic fact that a pronoun does not readily reveal its antecedent if it refers to a noun that is functioning in a subordinate structure such as a possessive (the **school's** principal), a modifier of a noun (the **school** term), or an object of a preposition (in the **school**). One remedy for the vague pronoun reference in sentence **4** is to use the noun **league** rather than the pronoun **it**: ". . . but the **league** could not enlist enough volunteers." Another remedy is to make **league** the subject of the first clause so that the **it** in the second clause would have an antecedent: "The **league** took as its first major step the sponsorship of a cleanup day, but **it** could not enlist enough volunteers."

25

An introductory verbal or verbal phrase must find its "doer" in the subject of the main clause.

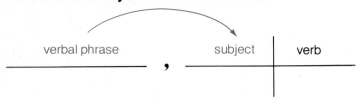

verbal phrase		subject	verb

Examples of "dangling" verbal phrases:

1 Revolving at a rate of 2200 revolutions per minute, the janitor turned off the overheated generator.
2 By stressing positive action, her inferiority complex can be eliminated.
3 Refusing to be inducted into the army, the World Boxing Association stripped Muhammad Ali of his title.
4 To pass the examinations, it is necessary for us to study diligently.

In English, an introductory verbal phrase (dominated by a participle, a gerund, or an infinitive) naturally adheres to the subject of the main clause. When the subject of the main clause is not the "doer" of the action indicated in the verbal, we say that the verbal **dangles**—that it is not attached to the proper agent. In each of the sentences above, the subject of the main clause is not the "doer" of the action specified by the introductory verbal (**revolving, stressing, refusing, to pass**).

To prevent dangling verbals, writers should make sure that the subject of the main clause is the doer of the action specified in the preceding verbal. If the authors of the sample sentences above had observed this caution, they would have revised their sentences to read as follows:

1 Revolving at the rate of 2200 revolutions per minute, the overheated generator was turned off by the janitor. **OR:** The janitor turned off the overheated generator, which was revolving at a rate of 2200 revolutions per minute.

2 By stressing positive action, she can eliminate her inferiority complex.

3 Refusing to be inducted into the army, Muhammad Ali was stripped of his title by the World Boxing Association. **OR:** The World Boxing Association stripped Muhammad Ali of his title for refusing to be inducted into the army.

4 To pass the examinations, we must study diligently.

Sometimes in revising our sentence to make the subject of the main clause the doer of the action specified in our introductory verbal, we have to resort to a rather awkward passive verb, as we did in revisions **1** and **3** above. In such cases, we may decide to recast the sentence so that it doesn't begin with a verbal phrase.

26

Misplaced modifiers lead to a misreading of the sentence.

Examples of misplaced modifiers:

1 Anyone who reads a newspaper **frequently** will notice that many people are now concerned about pollution.

2 He has **only** a face that a mother could love.

3 Matilda **even** smiles when she is sleeping.

4 The judge explained why traffic violations are a menace to society **on Tuesday**.

5 **After you entered the park**, the sponsors of the Summerfest de-

Grammar

cided that you would not have to spend any more money at the concession stands.

6 She paid $5.00 for a dress at the county fair **that she despised**.

Because English is a language that depends heavily on word order to protect meaning, related words, phrases, and clauses should be placed as close as possible to one another. Adverbial and adjectival modifiers especially must be placed as close as possible to words that they modify. Failure to juxtapose related words, phrases, or clauses may lead to a misreading—that is, to a reading different from what the author intended.

In sentence **1**, we have an example of what is called a **squinting modifier**, a modifier that looks in two directions at once. In that sentence, the adverb **frequently** sits between two verbs that it could modify—**reads** and **will notice**. If the writer intends the adverb to modify the act of *reading* rather than the act of *noticing*, the position of **frequently** should be shifted so that the sentence reads as follows: **Anyone who frequently reads a newspaper will notice that many people are now concerned about pollution**. If, however, the writer intends the adverb to modify the act of *noticing*, **frequently** should be shifted to a position between **will** and **notice** or after **notice**.

Because **only** in sentence **2** is placed in the wrong clause of the sentence, it modifies **a face**. The writer could avoid getting an unwanted laugh from readers by putting **only** in the clause where it belongs: **He has a face that only a mother could love**.

Chances are that the writer of sentence **3** did not intend **even** to modify the act of *smiling*. Shifting **even** will make the sentence say what the writer probably meant it to say: **Matilda smiles even when she is sleeping**.

Because the prepositional phrase **on Tuesday** has been put in the wrong place in sentence **4**, it does not modify the word that it should be modifying (**explained**) and therefore does not say what the writer intended to say. The sentence should be revised to read as follows: **The judge explained on Tuesday why traffic violations are a menace to society**.

Notice how shifting the position of the modifying clauses in sentences **5** and **6** makes the sentences say what they were probably intended to say:

> The sponsors of the Summerfest decided that after you entered the park you would not have to spend any more money at the concession stands.
>
> At the county fair, she paid $5.00 for a dress that she despised.

Reading sentences aloud will sometimes reveal the misplacement of modifying words, phrases, and clauses.

27

Preserve parallel structure by using units of the same grammatical kind.

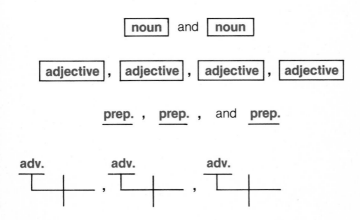

Grammar

Examples of breakdown in parallelism:

1 The old beliefs about theft have been rejected as **superstitions** and **detrimental** to one's prestige.

   (noun and adjective)

2 He was a **miser,** a **bachelor,** and **egotistical.**

   (noun, noun, adjective)

3 John was **healthy, wealthy,** and an **athlete.**

   (adjective, adjective, noun)

4 First of all, Daisy was an **adult, married,** and **had a young daughter.**

   (noun, adjective, verb phrase)

5 Lincoln was a man **of the people, for the people,** and **loved by the people.**

   (prepositional phrase, prepositional phrase, participial phrase)

6 The president commended the steelworkers **for their patriotism** and **because they did not ask for a wage increase.**

   (prepositional phrase, adverb clause)

7 I enjoy reading simply **for personal enlightenment** and **to develop mental sharpness.**

   (prepositional phrase, infinitive phrase)

8 The advertisers **not only** convince the reader that the Continental is a luxury car **but also** that the car confers status on its owner.

   (violation of parallelism with correlative conjunctions)

The principle governing parallel structure is that a pair or a series (three or more) of units serving the same function in a sentence should be composed of similar elements—e.g. nouns with nouns, adjectives with adjectives, not a mixture of nouns and adjectives. A breakdown in parallelism wrenches coherence because it disrupts the expectation that is set up for a reader when a series starts out with one kind of element and then shifts to another kind.

The obvious way to correct a breakdown in parallelism is to convert all the members of the pair or the series to units of the same grammatical kind. Let us first correct all the violations of parallelism in the sample sentences and then comment on the revisions.

1 The old beliefs about theft have been rejected as **superstitious** and **detrimental** to one's prestige.

   (adjective and adjective)

2 He was a **miser,** a **bachelor,** and an **egotist**.

   (noun, noun, noun)

3 John was **healthy, wealthy,** and **athletic**.

   (adjective, adjective, adjective)

4 First of all, Daisy was an **adult**, a married **woman**, and the **mother** of a young daughter.

   (noun, noun, noun)

5 Lincoln was a man **who was born of the people, who worked for the people,** and **who was loved by the people**.

   (adjective clause, adjective clause, adjective clause)

6 The president commended the steelworkers **for their patriotism** and **for their restraint**.

   (prepositional phrase, prepositional phrase)

7 I enjoy reading simply **to gain personal enlightenment** and **to develop mental sharpness**.

   (infinitive phrase, infinitive phrase)

8 The advertisers convince the reader not only **that the Continental is a luxury car** but also **that the car confers status on its owner**.

   (noun clause, noun clause)

In converting all the members of a pair or a series to units of the same grammatical kind, a writer sometimes has an either/ or choice available, but usually one of the options will be stylisti-

Grammar

cally preferable to the other. In sentences **2**, **6**, and **7**, the writer could have chosen another option:

2 He was **miserly, single,** and **egotistical**.

6 The president commended the steelworkers **because they were patriotic and because they did not ask for a wage increase**.

7 I enjoy reading simply **for personal enlightenment** and **for mental sharpness**.

Whenever alternative ways of repairing the breakdown in parallelism are available, the writer has to exercise judgment in deciding which is the better stylistic choice in a particular case.

Sentences **1**, **3**, and **4**, however, do not readily lend themselves to alternative revisions. In sentence **1**, for instance, the writer could convert the pair to two nouns (**superstitions** and **detriments**), but that wording is not as stylistically satisfactory as the conversion to two adjectives (**superstitious** and **detrimental**). The predicate terms in sentence **3** cannot be converted to three nouns because there are no single-word noun equivalents of the adjectives **healthy** and **wealthy**; so this sentence can be made parallel only by turning all three units into adjectives. The use of noun phrases was the only option available for the revision of sentence **4** because there is no noun or adjective equivalent of the verb phrase **had a young daughter**.

Correcting the violation of parallelism in sentence **5** was almost impossible because of the unavailability of three equivalent prepositional phrases or three equivalent participial phrases. The best that could be done in that case was to use three **who** clauses, but although that revision makes the sentence grammatically parallel, it is not stylistically satisfactory.

Sentence **8** illustrates a violation of parallelism when correlative conjunctions are used: **either . . . or; neither . . . nor; not (only) . . . but (also).** The principle operating with correlative conjunctions is that the same grammatical structure must be on the right-hand side of both conjunctions. We can more easily see the breakdown in parallelism if we lay out sentence **8** in two layers:

> The advertisers **not only** convince the reader that the Continental is a luxury car
> **but also** that the car confers status on its owner.

On the right-hand side of **not only**, the writer has this grammatical sequence: a verb (**convince**), a noun (**the reader**), and a noun clause (**that the Continental is a luxury car**). On the right-hand side of **but also**, however, the writer has *only* the noun clause (**that the car confers status on its owner**). The faulty parallelism can be revised in either of two ways:

> The advertisers **not only** convince the reader that the Continental is a luxury car
> **but also** convince the reader that the car confers status on its owner.

> The advertisers convince the reader **not only** that the Continental is a luxury car
> **but also** that the car confers status on its owner.

In both revisions, we now have the same grammatical structures on the right-hand side of both correlative conjunctions. But because the second revision has fewer words and less repetition than the first one, it is probably the better of the two revisions.

Note how parallelism is preserved in the following two sentences using correlative conjunctions:

> **Either** he will love the one and hate the other, **or** he will hate the one and love the other.
>
> He will **either** love the one and hate the other **or** hate the one and love the other.

Grammar

The principle governing parallelism: **like must be joined with like**.

28

Use the subordinate conjunction *that* if it will prevent a possible misreading.

Examples where it would be advisable to insert **that**:

1 My father believed ˄ his doctor, who was a boyhood friend, was wholly trustworthy.

2 A more realistic person would probably assert ˄ these statements about the ad were frivolous and sentimental.

3 He discovered ˄ the radio and the tape recorder in his roommate's closet had been stolen.

4 The author reported ˄ as soon as a Jew became intensely depressed in camp and lost all purpose for living, death came shortly after.

5 Professor Clements maintained ˄ communism rejected capitalism and ˄ democracy rejected collective ownership.

The tendency of any language is toward economy of means. So we omit syllables in such contractions as **he's, she'll, we'd, won't,** and we resort to such common elliptical expressions as **not all [of] the men; she is taller than I [am tall]; when [I was] in the fourth grade, I went to the zoo with my mother.** We also frequently omit the conjunction **that**, which introduces a noun clause serving as the object of a verb, as in "He said [**that**] he was going" and "He announced [**that**] I was a candidate for office."

Whether to use the conjunction **that** in written prose will be a problem only when a noun clause is being used as the direct object of a verb—but not in every instance of such use. If there is no chance that a sentence will be misread, it is all right, even in written prose, to omit **that**. But if there is a chance that a noun phrase following the verb may be read as the object of the verb rather than as the subject of the subsequent clause, then the writer can prevent even a momentary misreading by inserting **that** at the beginning of the noun clause. What follows may make all of this discussion clearer.

In a sentence like "He believed they were going," it is safe to omit **that** after **believed** because **they** cannot possibly be read as the object of **believed**. (If **they** were the object of the verb here, the pronoun would have to be **them—He believed them**.) But in a sentence like 1, it is not only possible but likely that the noun phrase **his doctor** will initially be read as the object of **believed** (he believed his doctor). Of course, as soon as readers come to the predicate **was wholly trustworthy**, they realize that they have misread the sentence, and so they have to back up and reread the sentence as the writer intended it to be read. But the writer could have prevented that initial misreading by inserting **that** after **believed—My father believed that his doctor, who was a boyhood friend, was wholly trustworthy**. Then the sentence can be read in only one way—the way in which the writer intended it to be read.

Read the other sample sentences aloud, the first time omitting **that**, the second time inserting **that** where the (∧) is. By doing this double reading of the sentences aloud, you will notice how the insertion of **that** ensures that the sentences will be read in the way the writer intended them to be read.

Whenever a reader has to reread a sentence in order to make sense of it, the writer is often the one to blame. Inserting **that** where it is necessary or advisable is one way to spare readers from having to reread a sentence.

29

Avoid the careless or indefensible use of sentence fragments.

Examples of questionable sentence fragments:

1 They tried to explain to the police that they intended to drive the brakeless car only two blocks to the repair shop. **Although they soon became aware that neither of the police officers was paying any attention to their explanation**.

2 **The reason for Holden's disappointment being that his sister wasn't there to comfort him**.

3 Both men are alike in that they try to help people if the effort does not result in too much trouble for themselves. **Herenger, in his idea that it is good to help someone with "so little trouble to himself," and the Baron, who believes in giving money to someone as long as there is no further responsibility involved**.

4 The bond between Gretta and Michael was strong enough to make him face death rather than be separated from her. **The tragedy here that such a love could not be consummated and that one so young should be cut off just at the dawn of life**.

5 I know what you're thinking. **The wife trying to maintain her stubborn pride, the husband feeling guilty and remorseful, the children looking desperately for somebody to reconcile their parents**.

A sentence fragment can be defined as a string of words, between an initial capital letter and a period or a question mark, that lacks a subject or a finite-verb predicate (or both) or that has a subject and a finite-verb predicate but is made part of a larger structure by a relative pronoun (**who, which, that**) or by a subordinating conjunction (**although, because, if, when,** etc.). (For a further discussion of the difference between a phrase and a clause and between an independent (main) clause and a dependent (subordinate) clause, see the LEGEND section at the front of the book.)

In example **1**, the string of words beginning with **although** and terminating with a period is a sentence fragment because although it has a subject (**they**) and a finite-verb predicate (**became**), it is turned into a dependent clause by the subordinating conjunction **although** at the beginning of it. If instead of using the subordinating conjunction **although**, the writer had used a coordinating conjunction (**but**) or a conjunctive adverb (**however**), the words that follow would be a complete sentence. But if **although** is used to begin that string of words, then the words must be made a part of the preceding independent clause:

> They tried to explain to the police that they intended to drive the brakeless car only two blocks to the repair shop, although they soon became aware that neither of the police officers was paying any attention to their explanation.

Example **2** is a sentence fragment because there is no finite-verb predicate for the noun **reason**. (There is a finite verb in the string—**wasn't**—but that verb is the predicate of the dependent noun clause **that his sister wasn't there to comfort him**.) There is a verbal here (the participle **being**), but by itself, that participle cannot serve as the predicate for **reason**. The simplest way to make that fragment a complete sentence is to convert the participle **being** into the finite verb **was**:

> The reason for Holden's disappointment was that his sister wasn't there to comfort him.

The boldface string of words in example **3** is a sentence fragment because neither **Herenger** nor **Baron**, both of which appear to be "subjects," has a predicate verb. By supplying the finite verb **believes** for both subjects, we can convert that fragment into an independent clause, which can stand by itself:

Grammar

Both men are alike in that they try to help people if the effort does not result in too much trouble for themselves. Herenger believes that it is good to help someone with "so little trouble to himself," and the Baron believes in giving money to someone as long as there is no further responsibility involved.

Apparently, the author of example **4** left out the verb in the boldface string of words, owing to mere carelessness. If the author had read the string aloud, he or she would probably have noticed that the predicate verb was missing. Simply putting in a verb like **was** will correct this sentence fragment:

The bond between Gretta and Michael was strong enough to make him face death rather than be separated from her. The tragedy here was that such a love could not be consummated and that one so young should be cut off just at the dawn of life.

Because example **5** lacks a predicate verb in the boldface string, it is difficult—if not impossible—for us readers to figure out what the relationship between the two groups of words is and therefore what the author was trying to say. Because we cannot figure out what the author was trying to say, we can only suggest possible revisions. The following revision is only one of a number of ways of rewriting the strings in order to eliminate the sentence fragment:

I know what you're thinking. You're thinking that the wife is trying to maintain her stubborn pride, the husband is feeling guilty and remorseful, and the children are looking desperately for somebody to reconcile their parents.

Whether a string of words constitutes a complete sentence or only a sentence fragment is a grammatical concern; whether the use of a sentence fragment is appropriate in a particular context and is therefore justifiable is a rhetorical or stylistic concern. It is a fact of life that we sometimes communicate with one another in sentence fragments. Take for instance the following exchange:

Where are you going tonight?
The movies.
Who with?
Jack.
Where?
The Palace.
What time?
About 8:30.
By car?
No, by bus.
Can I go?
Sure.

Once the context of that dialogue was established, both speakers communicated in fragments. Notice, though, that the dialogue had to be initiated by a complete sentence (the question **Where are you going tonight?**) and that later the first speaker had to resort again to a complete sentence **(Can I go?)** because there was no way to phrase that question clearly in a fragmentary way.

Native speakers of a language can converse in fragments because each of them is capable of mentally supplying what is missing from an utterance. When in response to the initial question the second speaker answers, **The movies**, that phrase conveys a meaning because the first speaker is able to supply, mentally and perhaps subconsciously, the missing elements in the fragmentary reply: **(I am going to) the movies.**

All of us have encountered sentence fragments in the written prose of some very reputable writers. Predicateless sentences are most likely to be found in mood-setting descriptive and nar-

Grammar

rative prose, as in this first paragraph of Charles Dickens's novel *Bleak House*:

> London. Michaelmas Term lately over, and the Lord Chancellor sitting in Lincoln's Inn Hall. Implacable November weather. As much mud in the streets, as if the waters had but newly retired from the face of the earth, and it would not be wonderful to meet a Megalosaurus, forty feet long or so, waddling like an elephantine lizard up Holborn Hill. Smoke lowering down from chimney-pots, making a soft black drizzle, with flakes of soot in it as big as full-grown snow-flakes—gone into mourning, one might imagine, for the death of the sun. Dogs, undistinguishable in mire. Horses, scarcely better; splashed to their blinkers. Foot passengers, jostling one another's umbrellas, in a general infection of illtemper, and losing their foothold at street-corners, where tens of thousands of other foot passengers have been slipping and sliding since the day broke (if this day ever broke), adding new deposits to the crust upon crust of mud, sticking at those points tenaciously to the pavement and accumulating at compound interest.

In that paragraph, there are a few clauses (that is, groups of words with a subject and a finite-verb predicate), but the paragraph consists primarily of nouns and noun phrases, some of them modified by participial phrases (e.g. **sitting in Lincoln's Inn Hall, splashed to their blinkers, jostling one another's umbrellas**). (It might be a good exercise for you to go through the paragraph and see if you can distinguish the sentence fragments from the complete sentences.) But although the passage is largely lacking in statements made with finite verbs, the sequence of sentence fragments does create effects that Dickens could not have achieved—or achieved as well—with complete sentences.

The points to be made in citing these examples of spoken and written discourse are (1) that sentence fragments are a part of the English language (in that sense, they are "grammatical''), (2) that in certain contexts they do communicate meaning, and (3) that in some circumstances and for some purposes they are appropriate and therefore acceptable, effective, and even stylistically desirable. But writers should be aware of what they are doing. They should be conscious that they are deliberately using a sentence fragment instead of a complete sentence; otherwise, they will be guilty of a *careless* use of a sentence fragment. And they should have some purpose or effect in mind when they use a sentence fragment; otherwise, they will be guilty of an *indefensible* use of a sentence fragment. In every case, they should be aware of the possibility that the sentence fragment may not communicate clearly with readers.

30

Independent clauses cannot be spliced simply with a comma.

Examples of comma splices:

1 We are not allowed to think for ourselves**,** that privilege is reserved for administrators.
2 The biggest government spender, according to *Time* magazine, is the Department of Agriculture**,** the next biggest spender is the Department of Defense.
3 Our minds are never challenged by the television set**,** it is just so much easier to sit there than to read a book.
4 The members of the city council are convinced of the need for wheelchair lifts on public buses**,** however, they can't figure out how the city or the bus companies could finance such equipment.

Grammar

A comma splice is the result of joining independent clauses with nothing but a comma. *A comma is a separating device, not a joining device.* A comma splice is, therefore, an error in punctuation, but since punctuation is, for the written language, the grammatical equivalent of vocal intonation in the spoken language, this error in punctuation can also be considered an error in grammar.

Independent clauses must be joined either by a coordinating conjunction (**and, but, or, for, nor, yet, so**) or by a semicolon. In addition to these two ways of properly splicing independent clauses, there are two other ways of fixing up a comma splice: by making separate sentences of the two clauses and by subordinating one of the clauses. Using each of these methods in turn, let us correct the comma splice in the first sample sentence above.

(a) Insert the appropriate coordinating conjunction after the comma:

We are not allowed to think for ourselves**,** **for** that privilege is reserved for administrators. •

(b) Substitute a semicolon for the comma:

We are not allowed to think for ourselves**;** that privilege is reserved for administrators.

(c) Subordinate one of the independent clauses:

We are not allowed to think for ourselves**,** **because** that privilege is reserved for administrators.

(d) Put a period at the end of the first independent clause and begin a new sentence with the first word of the second independent clause:

We are not allowed to think for ourselves**.** That privilege is reserved for administrators.

Although these four ways of repairing a comma splice are always available, one of them will usually be better in a particular instance. In sentence **1**, splicing the two clauses with a semi-colon would probably be best: **We are not allowed to think for ourselves; that privilege is reserved for administrators.** The semicolon here effects the closest union of the two related clauses and best points up the irony between the thoughts in the two clauses. We have made our choice of the semicolon on stylistic grounds; grammatically, the other three options are equally correct.

In the following revisions of the remaining sample sentences, we have corrected the comma splice by one of the four available methods, but it must be understood that each of the comma splices could have been corrected by one of the other three methods.

2 The biggest government spender, according to *Time* magazine, is the Department of Agriculture**, but** the next biggest spender is the Department of Defense.

3 Our minds are never challenged by the television set**.** It is just so much easier to sit there than to read a book.

4 **Although** the members of the city council are convinced of the need for wheelchair lifts on public buses, they can't figure out how the city or the bus companies could finance such equipment.

See **66** and **67** in the section on punctuation for the proper use of the semicolon.

31

Do not run independent clauses together without a conjunction or the proper punctuation.

Examples of independent clauses run together:

1 Why am I qualified to speak on this subject I just finished three dreadful years of high school.

2 Those shiny red apples sitting on my desk pleased me very much they were tokens of affection from my pupils.

3 Two suspects were arrested last week one of them was a cripple.

4 Leggatt was blackballed for having killed a man thus he would never be able to work on a ship again.

The term commonly used to label two or more independent clauses that have been run together without any conjunction or punctuation is **fused sentence** or **run-on sentence.** Fused sentences are not as common in writing as comma splices, but when they occur, they are even more of a stumbling block for a reader than comma splices are. If the writers of the sample sentences above had read their strings of words aloud, they would have detected a natural stopping place—a place where the expression of one thought ended and the expression of another began.

Once the writers had detected the fused sentence, they could then consider how best to revise it. Fused sentences can be corrected in the same four ways that comma splices can be corrected:

(a) Join the independent clauses with the appropriate coordinating conjunction:

Those shiny red apples sitting on my desk pleased me very much, **for** they were tokens of affection from my pupils.

(b) Splice the independent clauses with a semicolon:

Two suspects were arrested last week; one of them was a cripple.

(c) Subordinate one of the independent clauses:

Because Leggatt was blackballed for having killed a man, he would never be able to work on a ship again.

(d) Make separate sentences of the independent clauses:

Why am I qualified to speak on this subject? I just finished three dreadful years of high school.

As with comma splices, all four of these ways are usually available for correcting a fused sentence, but in a particular instance, one of them will probably be better than the others. Furthermore, some fused sentences do not readily lend themselves to correction by all four means. For instance, because sentence 1 fuses a question and a statement—**Why am I qualified to speak on this subject** (question) and **I just finished three dreadful years of high school** (statement)—it most readily lends itself to correction by the fourth method, that of making separate sentences of the two clauses. Sentence 3 does not readily lend itself to correction by the use of a coordinating conjunction. The coordinating conjunctions **or, nor, for, yet, so** just do not fit with the sense of the two clauses. Depending on the larger context in which the sentence occurred, joining the two independent clauses with the coordinating conjunctions **and** or **but** might work, but this way of revising the sentence would not be as satisfactory as joining the clauses with a semicolon.

Reading one's prose aloud will usually disclose instances where independent clauses have been run together.

Grammar

32

Choose words and put them together so that they make sense.

Examples of confused or puzzling sentences:

1 Much later in the story, the dinner conversation the function of the "small talk" seems to be about the old times.

2 The youth, rejected by his parents, by the world, by God, and tragically and ultimately he has rejected himself.

3 William Faulkner presents in his short story "Barn Burning" a human character that is as nonhuman as is feasible to a person's mind.

4 Now in the third stanza, the poet starts her descent. She brings about her conclusion of the boy, which can be paralleled to mankind.

5 Of course, this situation of rundown houses is not always the case, but instead the high rent that the tenants have to pay, which leaves little money for anything else.

A confused or puzzling sentence is one that because of some flaw in the *choice* of words or in the *arrangement* of words reveals no meaning or a scrambled meaning or a vague meaning. Unlike the stylistic flaws discussed in **40, 41,** and **42,** which produce vague or imprecise or inept sentences, this flaw of diction or arrangement produces what might be called a "non-English" sentence—a sentence that is semantically or grammatically impossible in the English language. For example, a sentence like "The ice cube froze" is a non-English sentence because of the choice of the semantically incompatible words **ice cube** and **froze.** (We can say, "The water froze," but we are uttering nonsense if we say, "The ice cube froze.") A sentence like "Harshly me teacher scolded the yesterday" is a non-English sentence because English grammar does not allow that arrangement of words. To make sense, those words would have to be arranged in an order like "The teacher scolded me harshly yesterday."

Some of the sample sentences are confused or puzzling mainly because of the choice of words. In sentence **3**, for example, there is some incompatibility between **human character** and **nonhuman,** and the word **feasible** simply does not fit in that context. In sentence **4**, the choice of **conclusion** produced the non-English phrase "her conclusion of the boy." The use of **paralleled** in the final clause of that sentence is an error in idiom, resulting in a non-English clause.

The other sample sentences are examples of confused or puzzling sentences produced by faulty syntax (arrangement of words). The writers of those sentences started out on a certain track but got derailed, or they switched to another track. Sentence **1**, for instance, starts out well enough—**Much later in the story, the dinner conversation. . .**—but then gets derailed. Sentence **2** starts out on one track and then switches to another.

If readers cannot figure out what the writer meant to say, they often cannot analyze what went wrong with the sentence, and they certainly cannot suggest how the bewildering sentence might be fixed up. The best they can do is to point out that the sentence makes no sense and urge the writer to rephrase it.

In the following revisions, (1) a guess has been made about what the author meant to say, (2) as many of the original words as possible have been retained, and (3) none of the needed stylistic changes has been made. We have merely tried to repair the sentences so that they make some kind of sense.

1 Much later in the story—during the dinner conversation—the function of the "small talk" seems to be to recall the old times.

Grammar

2 The youth, rejected by his parents, by the world, by God, has tragically and ultimately rejected himself.

3 William Faulkner presents in his short story "Barn Burning" a character that is as unlike a normal human being as a person could imagine.

4 Now in the third stanza, the poet starts her descent. She draws her conclusion about the boy, which is similar to the generalization that could be made about the rest of mankind.

5 Of course, the houses are not invariably rundown, but the high rent that the tenants have to pay leaves little money for anything else.

If reading sentences aloud to oneself does not help in detecting confused or puzzling sentences, it may be necessary to read them aloud to someone else.

33

Use the proper form of the verb.

Examples of the wrong form of the verb:

1 Before television came along, children **use** to read for hours by the fireplace.

2 Whenever I went shopping with my sister, I had the urge to buy everything I **seen.**

3 In that environment, it seemed that whatever you would **liked** to do was sinful.

4 Many parents never ask their children, "**Have** you **drank** your milk yet?"

5 Yesterday, when customers **lay** their umbrellas on the counter while paying their bills, they usually walked off without them.

6 When the incident at Three Mile Island occurred, many people **are frightened.**

7 On the top of the hill, there is a sturdy log cabin, which **was** three years old.

8 The *Delta Queen* **leaves** Davenport tomorrow. It **will arrive** in St. Louis on Tuesday, and it **stays** there for a day and a half.

Native speakers of English are often not aware of how subtly complicated the English verb system is, especially the system of tenses, which indicate the *time* of an action or a state of being. But foreigners who have to learn English in school are painfully aware of the subtleties of the verb system. English is doubly difficult for those foreigners whose native languages do not have a system of tenses for their verbs. Instead of indicating time by making some change in the *form* of the verb (e.g. **walk—walked; sleep—slept**), these languages indicate time by adding some *word* to the sentence—as English sometimes does to indicate future time even when the verb indicates present time (e.g. **She goes tomorrow**).

Native speakers of English, who learn the language in the natural way, as part of the normal process of growing up, usually handle the complicated verb system quite well. Occasionally, however, they use the wrong form of a verb, as did the writers of the sample sentences above. Let us analyze and correct the sample sentences and then review some of the basic conventions governing the formation of the past tense and the past participle of the English verb.

The omission of the **-d** at the end of **use** in a sentence like **1** above is understandable, because in speaking, we are scarcely conscious of pronouncing that final **-d**. But this expression must always be written as **used to**. The verb in sentence 4 (**drank**) has the past-tense form, but it should have the past-participle form (**drunk**) so that it will fit with its auxiliary verb **have**. The verb in the *when* clause of sentence **5** clearly needs to be put into the past tense, but the proper form of the past tense of the verb *lay* is **laid**.

Grammar

Of the three verbs in sentence **2**, one is in the wrong tense: **seen** should be **saw**. This mistake is the reverse of the situation in **4**. The verb in sentence **3** has a **-d** ending that should not be there: **liked** should be **like** (the reverse of **1**). The writer of that sentence may have been influenced to add the **-d** ending to **like** because of the other past-tense signals in the sentence (**seemed, would,** and **was**) or because of the sound of **t** in **to** (*like to = liket = liked*).

Sentences **6, 7,** and **8** illustrate the error known as **faulty sequence of tenses**—that is, a needless or an unjustifiable shift of tenses in successive clauses or sentences. In sentence **6**, the past tense (**occurred**) in the *when* clause is followed by an incompatible present tense (**are frightened**) in the main clause. Sentence **7** has a present tense (**is**) in the main clause and an unjustifiable past tense (**was**) in the adjective clause. In sentence **8**, there is a sequence of present tense (**leaves**), future tense (**will arrivè**), and present tense (**stays**). The context here seems to demand that all three verbs have the future-tense form. But one could also justify putting the three verbs in the present tense (**leaves, arrives, stays**).

Here now are all eight sample sentences with corrected verb forms:

1 Before television came along, children **used** to read for hours by the fireplace.

2 Whenever I went shopping with my sister, I had the urge to buy everything I **saw**.

3 In that environment, it seemed that whatever you would **like** to do was sinful.

4 Many parents never ask their children, "**Have** you **drunk** your milk yet?"

5 Yesterday, when customers **laid** their umbrellas on the counter while paying their bills, they usually walked off without them.

6 When the incident at Three Mile Island occurred, many people **were frightened**

7 On the top of the hill, there is a sturdy log cabin, which **is** three years old.

8 The *Delta Queen* **will leave** Davenport tomorrow. It **will arrive** in St. Louis on Tuesday, and it **will stay** there for a day and a half.

Most of the errors that writers make with verbs involve the lack of agreement in person or number between the subject and predicate or the wrong past-tense form or the wrong past-participle form. Subject-predicate agreement is dealt with in section **22**. This section has dealt mainly with improper past-tense and past-participle forms. The majority of English verbs form their past tense and past participle by adding **-ed** or **-d** to the stem form (e.g. **walk—walked; believe—believed**). These verbs are called *regular verbs* or sometimes *weak verbs*.

The so-called *irregular verbs* or *strong verbs* form their past tense and past participle by means of a change in spelling (e.g. **sing—sang—sung; hide—hid—hidden**). Most native speakers of English know the principal parts of most of these irregular verbs. When they do not know, or are not sure of, the principal parts, they consult a good dictionary, which regularly supplies the past tense and past participle of all irregular verbs. But for your convenience, here are the principal parts of some of the most commonly used irregular verbs. (Incidentally, the *stem form* of the verb is the form that combines with *to* to become the infinitive—**to walk, to go**; the stem form is also the form that the verb has when it is used with the first-person pronouns in the present tense—**I walk, we go**.)

Grammar

PRINCIPAL PARTS OF SOME IRREGULAR VERBS

stem form	past tense form	past-participle form
begin	began	begun
bite	bit	bitten
blow	blew	blown
break	broke	broken
choose	chose	chosen
do	did	done
drink	drank	drunk
drive	drove	driven
eat	ate	eaten
fall	fell	fallen
fly	flew	flown
forget	forgot	forgotten
give	gave	given
go	went	gone
know	knew	known
lay	laid	laid
lie	lay	lain
pay	paid	paid
ride	rode	ridden
ring	rang	rung
rise	rose	risen
run	ran	run
see	saw	seen
sit	sat	sat
speak	spoke	spoken
swear	swore	sworn
take	took	taken
throw	threw	thrown
wear	wore	worn

Style

Style is the result of the choices that a writer makes from the available vocabulary and syntactical resources of a language. A writer may not choose—or should not choose

- ☐ **Words and structures that are not part of the language:**

   The defendants have **klinded** the case to the Supreme Court.

   (no such word in the English language)

   All gas stations **have being closed** for the duration of the emergency.

   (no such verb structure in the English language)

- ☐ **Words and structures that make no sense:**

   The mountains lucidly transgressed sentient rocks.

   (a grammatical but nonsensical sentence)

- ☐ **Words and structures that do not convey a clear, unambiguous meaning:**

   The teacher gave the papers to the students that were chosen by the committee.

   *(was it the **papers** or the **students** that were chosen by the committee?)*

Style

Aside from these unavailable or inadvisable choices, however, the rich vocabulary and the flexible syntax of the English language offer the writer a number of alternative but synonymous ways of saying something. For instance, one may choose to use an active verb or a passive verb:

He reported the accident to the police.

OR

The accident was reported by him to the police.

Or one may shift the position of some modifiers:

He reported the accident to the police when he was ready.

OR

When he was ready, he reported the accident to the police.

Or one may substitute synonymous words and phrases:

He informed the police about the accident at the intersection.

OR

John notified Sergeant James Murphy about the collision at the corner of Fifth and Main.

A number of other stylistic choices may be open to the writer:

(a) whether to write a long sentence or to break up the sentence into a series of short sentences.

(long sentence)

In a sense, we did not have history until the invention of the alphabet, because before that invention, the records of national events could be preserved only if there were bards inspired enough to sing about those events and audiences patient enough to listen to a long, metered recitation.

OR

(a series of short sentences)

In a sense, we did not have history until the invention of the alphabet. Before that invention, the records of national events were passed on by singing bards. But those bards had to have audiences patient enough to listen to a long, metered recitation.

(b) whether to write a compound sentence or to subordinate one of the clauses.

(compound sentence)

None of the elegies that were delivered at funerals in eighteenth-century village churches have been preserved, but the "short and simple annals of the poor" have been preserved on thousands of gravestones from that era.

OR

(subordinate one of the clauses)

Although none of the elegies that were delivered at funerals in eighteenth-century village churches have been preserved, the "short and simple annals of the poor" have been preserved on thousands of gravestones from that era.

(c) whether to modify a noun with an adjective clause or with a participial phrase or merely with an adjective.

(adjective clause)

The house, which was painted a garish red, did not find a buyer for two months.

OR

(participial phrase)

The house, painted a garish red, did not find a buyer for two months.

OR

(adjective)

The garishly red house did not find a buyer for two months.

57

Style

(d) whether to use literal language or figurative language.

(literal)

The president walked into a room filled with angry reporters.

OR

(figurative)

The president walked into a hornet's nest.

(e) whether to use a "big" word or an ordinary word (*altercation* or *quarrel*), a specific word or a general word (*sauntered* or *walked*), a formal word or a colloquial word (*children* or *kids*).

(big, formal words)

Everyone was astonished by her phenomenal equanimity.

OR

(ordinary, colloquial words)

Everyone was flabbergasted by her unusual cool.

(f) whether to begin a succession of sentences with the same word and the same structure or to vary the diction and the structure.

(same word, same structure)

We wanted to preserve our heritage. We wanted to remind our children of our national heroes. We wanted to inspire subsequent generations to emulate our example.

OR

(different words, different structures)

We wanted to preserve our heritage. Our children, in turn, needed to be reminded of our national heroes. Could we inspire subsequent generations to emulate our example?

The availability of options such as these gives writers the opportunity to achieve variety in their style. *By varying the length, the rhythm, and the structure of their sentences, writers can avoid monotony, an attention-deadening quality in prose.* The previous sentence is a good example of the variety made possible by the availability of options. All the meanings packed into that sentence can be laid out in a series of short sentences. (Transformational grammarians refer to these "meanings" that are laid out in the "kernel sentences" as the *deep structure.* The *surface structure* of a sentence represents the choice of words and syntax that a writer uses to express that deep structure. Here is the deep structure of the sentence:

> Writers vary the length of their sentences.
> Writers vary the rhythm of their sentences.
> Writers vary the structure of their sentences.
> Writers can avoid monotony.
> Monotony in prose deadens the attention of readers.

One *could* choose precisely that succession of simple sentences as the surface structure to express the deep structure. Although these elementary sentences would be appropriate in a first-grade Dick-and-Jane reader, a succession of such monotonous sentences would soon turn adult readers away. By a series of transformations that involve **combining** (compounding), **embedding** (subordinating), **shifting** (rearranging), or **deleting** (omitting) the five sentences, one can produce a single neat sentence that emphasizes the main idea and holds the readers' attention. Here is one way that the writer might have chosen to express the deep structure:

> If writers vary the length, the rhythm, and the structure of their sentences, they can avoid monotony, which deadens readers' attention.

Style

The writer of the first sentence (in italics) chose to combine some of the same elements combined by the writer of the sentence immediately above—e.g. compounding the "meanings" of the first three kernel sentences. On the other hand, the first writer chose a different way of embedding some of the elements—e.g. instead of using the adverbial *if* clause, the writer used an *-ing* gerund phrase (**varying**); and instead of using the adjectival *which* clause, the writer reduced the clause, by a series of deletions of words, to a compound adjective (**attention-deadening**). So instead of

> If writers vary the length, the rhythm, and the structure of their sentences, they can avoid monotony, which deadens readers' attention.

we get

> By varying the length, the rhythm, and the structure of their sentences, writers can avoid monotony, an attention-deadening quality in prose.

By using a different combination of combining, embedding, shifting, and deleting, other writers would come up with other ways of expressing all the meanings. The different ways result in different styles.

Choice is the key word in connection with style. Some choices a writer may not, or should not, make. As was pointed out at the beginning of this section, a writer may not choose what the grammar of the language does not allow. Furthermore, a writer cannot choose resources of language he or she does not command. A writer would also be ill-advised to choose words and structures that are inappropriate for the subject matter, the occasion, or the audience.

Aside from those constraints, however, a writer has hundreds of decisions to make about the choice of vocabulary or syntax while writing. Grammar will determine whether a particular stylistic choice is *correct*—that is, whether a particular locution complies with the conventions of the language. Rhetoric will determine whether a particular stylistic choice is *effective* —that is, whether a particular locution conveys the intended meaning with the clarity, economy, emphasis, and tone appropriate to the subject matter, occasion, audience, and desired effect.

The previous section dealt with what the grammar of the language permits—or, more accurately, with what the conventions of Edited American English permit. This section on style will guide writers in making judicious choices from among the available options. Questions about style are not so much questions about *right* and *wrong* as questions about *good, better, best*.

40

Choose the right word or expression for what you intend to say.

Examples of wrong words or expressions:

1 If you do not **here** from me within three weeks, give me a call.

2 The shortstop played very **erotically** in the first game of the double-header.

3 The typical surfer has long **ignominious** hair bleached by the **torpid** sun.

4 A thief and a liar **are vices** that we should avoid.

5 Abused children **should not be tolerated** in our society.

6 The source of Hemingway's title **is taken** from a sermon by John Donne.

7 The reason she didn't come to class **is because** she was sick.

Style

8 The beach **is where** I get my worst sunburn.

9 An example of honesty **is when** someone finds a wallet and brings it to the police.

A word is labeled "wrong" when it does not express the author's intended meaning. The most obvious instance of a "wrong word" is the substitution, usually due to carelessness, of a homonym (a like-sounding word) for the intended word—e.g. **through** for **threw, there** for **their, sole** for **soul, son** for **sun, loose** for **lose**. Sentence 1 has one of these homonyms —**here** for **hear**.

Another kind of "wrong word" is called a **malapropism**, after Mrs. Malaprop in Sheridan's play *The Rivals*. Mrs. Malaprop would say things like "as headstrong as an *allegory* on the banks of the Nile," when she should have used the word *alligator*. There is a malapropism in sentence 2. "Played erratically" is a common phrase, but by using the approximate-sounding word **erotically** in that phrase, the writer has produced a howler.

The occurrence of a "wrong word" is commonly the result of a writer's using a word that is new and somewhat unfamiliar to him or her. In sentence 3, the word *ignominious* is wrong for that context. The denotative meaning of the word is "disgraceful," "shameful," but although we can speak of "an ignominious act," the word is "wrong" when applied to **hair**. In the same sentence, if the writer meant to say that the sun was sluggish, **torpid** is the right word; but "torrid sun" comes closer to what the writer probably intended to say.

Wrong words commonly occur as part of the predication of a sentence. This fault is so common that it has acquired its own label—**faulty predication**. A faulty predication occurs when the predicate of a clause (either the verb itself or the whole verb phrase) does not fit semantically or syntactically with the subject of the clause.

40 Wrong Word and Faulty Predication

Sentences **4**, **5**, and **6** illustrate a semantic mismatch between the subject and the predicate. Thieves and liars cannot be called vices; *thievery* and *lies* are vices. Sentence **5** says that we should not tolerate abused children. Probably what the writer meant to say is that the abuse of children should not be tolerated. In sentence **6**, the predicate **is taken** is incompatible with the subject **source**. It was the title, not the source, that was taken from Donne's sermon.

Sentences **7**, **8**, and **9** illustrate common instances of faulty predication involving a syntactical mismatch between the subject and the predicate. The adverb clauses in those sentences cannot serve as complements for the verb **to be**. (No more could a simple adverb serve as the complement of the verb **to be**: "he is swiftly.") One way to correct such faulty predications is to put some kind of nominal structure after the **to be** verb—a noun, a noun phrase, or a noun clause. Avoid this kind of predication:

The reason is because . . .

An example is when . . .

A ghetto is where . . .

Here are the revisions of the "wrong word" sentences:

1 If you do not hear from me within three weeks, give me a call.

2 The shortstop played very erratically in the first game of the double-header.

3 The typical surfer has long, stringy hair bleached by the torrid sun.

4 A thief and a liar practice vices that we should avoid.

5 The abuse of children should not be tolerated in our society.

6 The source of Hemingway's title is a sermon by John Donne.

7 The reason she didn't come to class is that she was sick.

8 The beach is the place where I get my worst sunburn.

9 Honesty is the virtue exemplified when someone finds a wallet and brings it to the police.

Style

41

Choose the precise word for what you want to say.

Examples of imprecise words:

1 I liked the movie *Breaking Away* because it was **interesting.**
2 What most impressed me about the poem was the poet's **descriptive** language.
3 Has-been athletes always have a **sore** look on their face.
4 To prevent her from catching a cold, he insisted that she wear the **gigantic** galoshes.
5 Honesty is a **thing** that we should value highly.
6 Jane sold her car, **as** she was planning to take a trip to Europe.

Whereas a "wrong word" misses the target entirely, an "imprecise word" hits all around the bull's-eye and never on dead center. But the governing principle here is that one should strive only for as much precision in diction as the situation demands.

In the spoken medium, diction is often imprecise. But fortunately, in many conversational situations, our diction does not have to be sharply precise in order to communicate adequately. In a conversation, for instance, if someone asked, "How did you like him?" we might respond, "Oh, I thought he was very nice." The word *nice* does not convey a precise meaning, but for the particular situation, it may be precise enough. The word *nice* here certainly conveys the meaning that we approve of the person, that we are favorably impressed by the person. In speech, we do not have the leisure to search for the words that express our meaning exactly. If the woman who asked the question were not satisfied with our general word of approval, *nice*, she could ask us to be more specific.

In the written medium, however, we do have the leisure to search for a precise word, and we are not available to the reader who may want or need more specific information than our words supply. Generally, the written medium requires that the words we choose be as exact, as specific, as unequivocal as we can make them. Consulting a thesaurus or, better yet, a dictionary that discriminates the meanings of synonyms will frequently yield the word that conveys our intended meaning precisely.

The word **interesting** in sentence 1 is too general to convey a precise meaning. A reader's response to a general word like that would be to ask, "In what way was the movie interesting?" If the writer had said "innovative" or "spellbinding" or "thought-provoking," readers might want some more particulars, but at least they would have a clearer idea of the sense in which the writer considered the movie to be interesting.

The word **descriptive** in sentence 2 is too vague. Expressions like "the poet's simple, concrete words" or "the poet's specific adjectives for indicating colors" would give readers a more exact idea of the kind of descriptive language that impressed the writer of the sentence.

Sore in sentence 3 is ambiguous—that is, it has more than one meaning in its context. The word **sore** could mean either "angry, disgruntled" or "aching, painful." The choice of a more exact word here will clarify the writer's meaning.

Gigantic in sentence 4 above is exaggerated. Unless the word were deliberately chosen to create a special effect of humor or irony, the writer should use a word more proportionate to the circumstances, such as *big* or *heavy* or *ungainly*.

In the oral medium, we can get by with a catchall word like **thing**, as in sentence 5, but writing allows us the leisure to search for a word that will serve as a more accurate predicate complement for *honesty*. We can use words like *policy, virtue, habit, disposition*—whichever fits best with what we want to say about honesty here.

Style

The subordinating conjunction **as** carries a variety of meanings, and it is not always possible to tell from the context which of its several meanings it carries in a particular sentence. In sentence **6**, we cannot tell whether **as** is being used in its sense of "because" or "since" or "when" or "while." We should use the conjunction that exactly expresses our intended meaning: **because** she was planning; **when** she was planning; **while** she was planning. We should reserve the conjunction **as** for those contexts in which there is no possibility of ambiguity, as in sentences like "In that kind of situation, he acts exactly **as** he should" and "Do **as** I say."

Here, for each of the sample sentences, is one possible revision for greater precision:

1 I liked the movie *Breaking Away* because the theme was poignant.
2 What most impressed me about the poem was the poet's vivid, sensory diction.
3 Has-been athletes always have a disgruntled look on their face.
4 To prevent her from catching a cold, he insisted that she wear the big galoshes.
5 Honesty is a virtue that we should value highly.
6 Jane sold her car, because she was planning to take a trip to Europe.

42

Choose words that are appropriate to the context.

Examples of inappropriate words:

1 He didn't want to **exacerbate** his mother's **sangfroid,** so he **indited** an **epistolary message** to inform her of his unavoidable **retardation.**

2 Whenever I visit a new city, I browse through a secondhand book-store and eventually **cheapen** a book.

3 The conclusion that I have come to is that **kids** should not have to suffer for the sins of their fathers.

4 Merchants in areas where the freeway would be built have persist-ently opposed the project, claiming that it would disturb the residents and **freak out** all the **weirdos** in the area.

A word is inappropriate if it does not fit, if it is out of tune with, the subject matter, the occasion, the audience, or the personality of the writer. It is a word that is conspicuously "out of place" with its environment.

No word in isolation can be labeled inappropriate; it must first be seen in the company of other words. Although one would feel safer in making a judgment if one had a larger context, the boldfaced words in the sample sentences above seem to be inappropriate.

Sentence **1** exhibits the kind of language used by (usually beginning) writers who are passing through a phase in which they seem unable to say even a simple thing in a simple way. Young writers consciously striving to enlarge their vocabulary often produce sentences like this one. Instead of using a thesaurus to find an accurate or precise word, they use it to find an unusual or polysyllabic word that they think will make their prose sound "literary" or learned or both. Fortunately, most of those who are ambitious enough to want to expand their working vocabulary develop eventually enough sophistication to be able to judge when their language is appropriate and when it is not.

Sentence **2** illustrates another kind of inappropriateness. The word **cheapen** was once a perfectly appropriate word as used in this context. During the Elizabethan period in England, it was a common verb meaning "to bid for," "to bargain for." If you look up the word in a modern dictionary, you will discover that

Style

cheapen in this sense is labeled archaic. The label means that the word in that sense can no longer be used in a modern context.

The more common fault of inappropriateness, however, is diction that is too colloquial or too slangy for its context. This fault is illustrated in sentences **3** and **4**. Although there are contexts in which the colloquial word **kids** would be more appropriate than the word *children*, sentence **3** seems not to be one of those contexts. There are contexts where slang and even the jargon of particular social groups would be perfectly appropriate, but the slang in sentence **4** seems to be out of tune with the subject matter and with almost all of the other words in the sentence.

Since dictionaries, thesauruses, and handbooks will not be of much help in telling a writer that a word is inappropriate, the writer will have to rely on the criteria of subject matter, occasion, audience, desired effect, and personality of the author. Another way of putting this precept is to say that the writer's "voice" must remain in harmony with the overall tone that he or she has established in a particular piece of writing.

Here are some revisions of the sample sentences, with more appropriate diction:

1 He didn't want to upset his mother, so he wrote her a note to inform her that he would be late.

2 Whenever I visit a new city, I browse through a secondhand bookstore and eventually bid for a book.

3 The conclusion that I have come to is that children should not have to suffer for the sins of their fathers.

4 Merchants in areas where the freeway would be built have persistently opposed the project, claiming that it would disturb the residents and disconcert the eccentric transients in the area.

43

Use the proper idiom.

Examples of lapse of idiom:

1 Although I agree **to** a few of Socrates' principles, I must disagree **to** many of them.
2 Formerly devoted **on** a theatrical career, she developed a strong passion **in** gourmet cooking.
3 Conformity has been a common tendency throughout **the** American history.
4 Nobody seems immune **from** pressures.
5 It's these special characters and their motives that I intend **on concentrating** in this paper.
6 Abner had no interest or respect **for** the boy.

To label a locution unidiomatic is to indicate that native speakers of the language do not say it that way—in any dialect of the language. Unidiomatic expressions are one of the commonest weaknesses to be found in the prose of unpracticed writers. Why do lapses of idiom occur so frequently? That is a good question to ask, because writers presumably do not hear other native speakers use the curious expressions that they write down on paper. One explanation for the frequency of idiomatic lapses is that in writing, unpracticed writers use words and structures that they seldom or never use in speech; and because they have not paid close enough attention to the way native speakers say something, they make a guess—usually a wrong guess—at how the expression should be phrased.

No word by itself is ever unidiomatic. Only combinations of words can be unidiomatic. The commonest kind of idiomatic lapse is the one that occurs with a preposition. Three of the first four sample sentences above involve idiomatic lapses in the use of prepositions.

A number of prepositions fit idiomatically with the verbs **agree** and **disagree**, but the preposition that fits idiomatically with the sense of **agree** and **disagree** in sentence 1 is **with**. There will be other contexts when the correct preposition to use with **agree** will be **to** ("They agreed to the conditions we laid down") or **on** ("They can't agree on the wording of the proposal").

There are two unidiomatic prepositions in sentence 2. Native speakers don't say "devoted **on**" or "a passion **in**"; they say "devoted **to**" and "a passion **for**." In a sentence like 4, above, native speakers don't say "immune **from**"; they say "immune **to**."

No native speaker of English would use the article **the** in the phrase **throughout the American history** (see sentence 3). However, an American speaker would say, "He was in the hospital," whereas a British speaker would say, "He was in hospital." Some Asian speakers have trouble with the English article, because their language does not use a part of speech like it.

Sentence 5 above is clearly an instance of a writer's using a structure that he or she has never attempted before and failing to recall how native speakers phrase it. The structure should be phrased in this way: "intend **to concentrate on**."

Unidiomatic expressions often appear in compounded phrases, as in sentence 6. The preposition **for** fits with **respect** ("respect **for** the boy"), but it does not fit with **interest** (not "interest **for** the boy" but "interest **in** the boy"). In such cases, the idiomatic preposition must be inserted for both members of the compound (see the revision below).

What prevents a handbook from setting reliable guidelines for proper idiom is the fact that logic plays little or no part in establishing the idioms of a language. If logic were involved in establishing idioms, we would say, "He looked *down* the word in the dictionary" instead of what we do say, "He looked *up* the word in the dictionary." Likewise, the logical preposition to use with the verb **center** is **on**—"Her efforts centered on community service." But more and more, usage seems to be establishing the idiom of **around** with **center**—"Her efforts centered around community service." Editors or teachers can call your attention to an unidiomatic expression and can insert the correct idiom, but they cannot give you any rule that will prevent other lapses of idiom. You simply have to learn proper idioms by reading more and by listening more intently.

Here are the revisions of the unidiomatic expressions:

1 Although I agree **with** a few of Socrates' principles, I must disagree **with** many of them.

2 Formerly devoted **to** a theatrical career, she developed a strong passion **for** gourmet cooking.

3 Conformity has been a common tendency throughout American history.

4 Nobody seems immune **to** pressures.

5 It's these special characters and their motives that I intend **to concentrate on** in this paper.

6 Abner had no interest **in,** or respect **for,** the boy.

44

Avoid trite expressions.

Examples of trite expressions:

1 I returned from the picnic **tired but happy,** and that night **I slept like a log.**

Style

2 My primary objective in coming to college was to get a **well-rounded education.**

3 The construction of two new hotels was a **giant step forward** for the community.

4 In the last few years, the popularity of ice hockey has grown **by leaps and bounds.**

5 Convinced now that drugs are a temptation for young people, the community must **nip the problem in the bud** before it **runs rampant.**

There is nothing grammatically or idiomatically wrong with a trite expression. A trite expression is *stylistically* objectionable—mainly because it is a *tired* expression. Whether an expression is "tired" is, of course, a relative matter. What is lackluster for some readers may be bright-penny new for others. But it would be surprising if the expressions in the examples above were not jaded for most readers.

Trite expressions are certain combinations of words or certain figures of speech that have been used so often that they have lost their freshness and even their meaning for most readers. Rhetorically, the price that writers pay for their use of trite language is the alienation of their readers. Readers stop paying attention. Writers may have something new and important to say, but if their message is delivered in threadbare language, they will lose or fail to capture the attention of their readers.

Figures of speech are especially prone to staleness. Metaphors like "nip in the bud," "slept like a log," "giant step" were once fresh and cogent; they are now wilted from overuse. Trite combinations of words like "tired but happy," "by leaps and bounds," "runs rampant" produce glazed-eyed readers. Ironically, one of the ways in which to revise sentences that have trite language is to use the most familiar, ordinary language. Sentence **1**, for example, would be improved if the **but happy** part of the combination were dropped and if a simple adverb were substituted for the simile **like a log**:

I returned from the picnic tired, and that night I slept soundly.

Sometimes, making a daring alteration in a tired expression can rejuvenate the sentence. Look at what happens to the yawn-producing **well-rounded education** in this revision of sentence 2:

My primary objective in coming to college was to get a well-squared education.

If you make an effort to invent your own figures of speech, you may produce awkward, strained figures, but at least they will be fresh. Instead of borrowing the hackneyed metaphor **nip the problem in the bud**, make up your own metaphor:

Convinced now that drugs are a temptation for young people, the community should excise the tumor before it becomes a raging cancer.

It takes a great deal of sophistication about language even to recognize trite expressions, and those who don't read very much can hardly be expected to detect tired language, because almost all the expressions that they encounter are relatively new to them. They may have to rely on others to point out the trite language in their prose.

Be wary of weary words.

45

Rephrase awkwardly constructed sentences.

Examples of awkward sentences:

1 You could get a dose of the best exercise a person could undertake,

walking. I believe a person should walk at a leisurely pace, with no set goal on distance.

2 The football player has had many broken noses, with which he ends up looking like a prizefighter.

3 I and probably everybody else who started drinking beer in their sophomore year of high school thought the only thing to do was get drunk and go to school activities where we could meet and have a good time.

The fault dealt with in **32**, in the Grammar section, concerns sentences that are so badly put together that they reveal no meaning or only a vague meaning. Awkward sentences, which are dealt with in this section, are sentences so ineptly put together that they are difficult—but not impossible—for readers to understand. They are sentences that are grammatically passable but stylistically weak.

The problem is that those who write awkwardly constructed sentences are usually not aware that they are doing so; they have to be told that their sentences are awkward. The ear, however, is a reliable resource for detecting awkward sentences. If writers adopt the practice of reading their sentences aloud, they will often detect clumsy, odd-sounding combinations of words. Thus alerted, they can then examine their sentences for the presence of any of the usual causes of awkwardness:

(a) Excessive number of words (see sentence **3**)

(b) Words and phrases out of their normal order (note the position of **walking** in sentence **1**)

(c) Successions of prepositional phrases ("the president of the largest chapter of the national fraternity of students of dentistry")

(d) Pretentious circumlocutions ("the penultimate month of the year" for "November")

(e) Split constructions ("I, chastened by my past experiences, resolved to never consciously and maliciously circulate, even if true, damaging reports about my friends")

(f) Successions of rhyming words ("She tries wisely to revise the evidence supplied by her eyes")

In rephrasing awkward sentences, writers might try expressing the same thoughts in the way they would if they were *speaking* the sentences to others. These spoken versions might need some further touching up, but they probably would no longer be awkward. For example, the phrasing "the president of the largest fraternity chapter of dental students" gets rid of two of the four prepositional phrases that were in the original version (c). Shifting the word order gets rid of some of the awkwardness caused by the split constructions (d): "Chastened by my past experiences, I resolved never to circulate damaging reports about my friends consciously and maliciously, even if they were true." Choosing synonymous words eliminates the series of rhyming words (f): "She attempts a judicious alteration of the evidence presented by her eyes." A writer might still want to polish those sentences further, but whatever other faults those revisions still have, at least the awkwardness has been removed.

The sample sentences at the beginning of this section are awkward for a variety of reasons, but what they all have in common is wordiness. Pruning some of the deadwood, rearranging some of the parts, using simpler, more idiomatic phrases, we can improve the articulation of those clumsy sentences:

1 Walking is the best exercise. A person should walk at a leisurely pace and only as far as he feels like going.

2 The football player has broken his nose so often that he looks like a prizefighter.

3 Like everybody else who started drinking beer as a high-school

sophomore, I thought that getting drunk and going to school activities would be the best way to ensure a good time.

Construct your sentences so smoothly that your readers won't have to stumble through them.

46

Cut out unnecessary words.

Examples of wordy sentences:

1 He was justified in trying to straighten out his mother on her backward ideas about her attitude toward blacks.
2 In this modern world of today, we must get an education that will prepare us for a job in our vocation in life.
3 In the "Garden of Love," the poem relates the sad experience of a child being born into a cruel world.
4 The meaning, at least in my own eyes, that he is trying to convey in the poem "Arms and the Boy" is of the evilness of war in that it forces innocent people to take up the instruments of death and destruction and then tries to teach them to love to use them to kill other human beings.
5 These rivers do not contain fish, due to the fact that the flow of water is too rapid.

A "wordy sentence" is one in which a writer has used more words than are needed to say what has to be said. The superfluous words simply clutter up a sentence and impede its movement. Speakers are especially prone to verbosity because words come so easily to their tongues. But writers too are prone to verbosity once they acquire a certain facility with words. Facile writers have to make a conscious effort to control their expenditure of words. Writers would soon learn to cultivate restraint if they were charged for every word used, as they are when they send a telegram. They should not, of course, strive for a "telegraphic" or a "headline" style, but they should learn to value words so much that they spend words sparingly.

Let us see if we can trim the sample sentences without substantially altering their meaning:

1 He was justified in trying to straighten out his mother's attitude toward blacks. (from 19 to 13 words)

2 In the modern world, we must get an education that will prepare us for a job. (from 23 to 13 words)

3 The "Garden of Love" relates the sad experience of a child born into a cruel world. (from 20 to 16 words)

4 As I see it, the poet's thesis in "Arms and the Boy" is that war is evil because it not only forces people to take up arms but makes them use these weapons to kill other human beings. (from 58 to 38 words)

5 These rivers do not contain fish, because they flow too rapidly. (from 18 to 11 words)

Each of the revised sentences uses fewer words than the original. The retrenchment ranges from four words to twenty words. If the writers were being charged a quarter a word, they could probably find other superfluous words to prune. The writer of the fourth sentence, for instance, would lop off **As I see it** and would condense **to kill other human beings** to **to kill others**.

One should not become obsessed with saving words, but one should seize every opportunity, in the revising stage, to clear out obvious deadwood. As Alexander Pope said,

> Words are like leaves, and where they most abound,
> Much fruit of sense beneath is rarely found.

Style

47

Avoid careless or needless repetition of words and ideas.

Examples of careless or needless repetition:

1 Mrs. Bucks, a **fellow colleague**, offered to intercede with the dean.

2 He does not rely on the **surrounding environment** as much as his sister does.

3 The objective point of view accentuates the emotional intensity of the love affair and the **impending** failure that will **eventually happen**.

4 **In Larry's mind** he **thinks**, "I have never met anyone so absorbed in himself."

5 There are some striking similarities between Segal and Hemingway, for **both** have studied life and love and found them **both** to be failures.

6 After **setting** up camp, we **set** off to watch the sun **set**.

A "careless or needless repetition" refers either to the recurrence of a word in the same sentence or in adjoining sentences or to the use of synonymous words that produces what is called a **redundancy** or a **tautology**.

The emphasis in this caution about repetition should be put on the words *careless* and *needless*, for there are cases where repetition serves a purpose. Item **51** in the next section, for instance, shows that the repetition of key words can be an effective means of achieving coherence in a paragraph. Sometimes too it is better to repeat a word, even in the same sentence, than to run the risk of ambiguity or misunderstanding. In the first sentence of this paragraph, for example, the word **repetition** has been repeated because the use of the pronoun *it* in place of **repetition** would be ambiguous ("The emphasis in this caution about repetition should be put on the words *careless* and *needless*, for there are cases where **it** serves a purpose'').

The boldfaced words in the first four examples above are instances or redundancy or tautology (needless repetition of the same idea in different words). **Fellow** and **colleague, surrounding** and **environment, impending** and **eventually happen** are examples of needless repetition. In sentence **4**, the phrase **In Larry's mind** is superfluous (where else does one **think** but in the mind?). The repetition of the pronoun **both** in sentence **5** is especially careless because the repeated pronouns have different antecedents (the first one refers to **Segal** and **Hemingway**, the second to **life** and **love.** In sentence **6**, we have an instance of the same basic verb form (**set**) repeated in three different senses.

Here are revisions of the sample sentences to eliminate the repetitions:

1 Mrs. Bucks, a **colleague,** offered to intercede with the dean.

2 He does not rely on the **environment** as much as his sister does.

3 The objective point of view accentuates the emotional intensity of the love affair and its **impending** failure.

4 Larry **thinks**, "I have never met anyone so absorbed in himself."

5 There are some striking similarities between Segal and Hemingway, for both of them have studied life and love and found them to be failures.

6 After preparing camp, we took off to watch the sun set.

48

Avoid mixed metaphors.

Examples of mixed metaphors:

1 Sarty finally comes to the point where his inner turmoil reaches its **zenith** and **stagnates in a pool** of lethargy.

2 In "The Dead," James Joyce uses small talk as an effective **weapon** to **illustrate** his thesis.

3 She tried to **scale the wall** of indifference between them but found that she couldn't **burrow** through it.

4 The experience struck a **spark** that **massaged** the poet's imagination.

5 When we tried to get the mayor's campaign **off the ground,** we found that his campaign **sank in a sea** of indifference.

A mixed metaphor is the result of a writer's failure to keep a consistent image in mind. All metaphors are based on the perceived likenesses between things that exist in different orders of being—as for instance between a *man* and a *greyhound* ("The lean shortstop is a greyhound when he runs the bases"), *fame* and a *spur* ("Fame is the spur to ambition"), *mail* and an *avalanche* ("The mail buried the staff under an avalanche of complaints"). Whenever any detail is incompatible with one or other of the terms of the analogy, the metaphor is said to be mixed.

   Zenith, in sentence **1**, connotes something rising to its highest point, and therefore that image of ascending motion is incompatible with the detail of **stagnation**. Likewise, a **weapon** is not used to **illustrate** something. If one were climbing (**scaling**) a wall, one could not dig (**burrow**) through it at the same time. A **spark** could start a fire, but it couldn't **massage** anything. The basic metaphor in the first half of the fifth sentence above is that of an airplane taking off, but in the second half of the sentence, the metaphor shifts to that of a ship sinking.

The following revisions unscramble the mixed metaphors:

1 Sarty finally comes to the point where his inner turmoil reaches its **zenith** and **fizzles out** into lethargy.

2 In "The Dead," James Joyce uses small talk as a **mirror** to **reflect** his thesis.

3 She tried to **scale the wall** of indifference between them but found that she couldn't **surmount** it.

4 The experience struck a **spark** that **ignited** the poet's imagination.

5 When we tried to get the mayor's campaign **off the ground**, we found that the campaign didn't **get up enough speed** to become **airborne**

Forming and maintaining a clear picture of the notion one is attempting to express figuratively will ensure a consistent metaphor.

49

Consider whether an active verb would be preferable to a passive verb.

Examples of questionable use of the passive voice:

1 Money **was borrowed** by the couple so that they could pay off all their bills.

2 His love for her **is shown** by his accepting her story and by his remaining at her side when she is in trouble.

3 From these recurrent images of hard, resistant metals, it **can be inferred** by us that she was a mechanical, heartless person.

4 Talking incessantly, he **was overwhelmed** by the girl.

Style

The passive voice of the verb is a legitimate and useful part of the English language. A sentence using a passive verb as its predicate is a different but synonymous way of expressing the thought conveyed by a sentence using an active verb. The basic formula for a sentence using an active-verb construction is as follows:

NOUN PHRASE₁ + VERB + NOUN PHRASE₂

The judge   pronounced   the verdict

The formula for transforming that active-verb construction into a passive-verb construction is as follows:

NOUN PHRASE₂ + AUXILIARY + VERB (past participle form) + **by** + NOUN PHRASE₁

The verdict   was   pronounced   by   the judge

Notice the changes that have taken place in the second sentence: (1) Noun Phrase₁ and Noun Phrase₂ have switched positions, and (2) two words have been added, the auxiliary **was** and the preposition **by.** Although the second sentence expresses the same thought as the first sentence, it is longer, by two words, than the first sentence.

If the use of a passive verb is questionable, it is questionable stylistically, not grammatically. To question the use of a passive verb is to ask the writer to consider whether the sentence would not be more emphatic or more economical or less awkward or somehow "neater" if an active verb were used. Challenged to consider the options available in a particular case, the writer is the final judge of the best choice in that case.

Writers sometimes decide to use the passive verb because they want to give special emphasis to some word in the sentence. In sentence **1**, the word **money** gets special emphasis because it occupies the initial position. If the active verb were used, the word **couple** would get the special emphasis. It would be more difficult to cite emphasis as the justification for the choice of passive verbs in sentences **2** and **3**. Writers can also justify the use of a passive verb when they do not know the agent of an action or prefer not to reveal the agent or consider it unnecessary to indicate the agent, as in the sentence "The story was reported to all the newspapers."

Dangling verbals often result from the use of a passive verb in the main clause of the sentence (see **25** on dangling verbals). The context of sentence **4** suggests that the lead-off participial phrase (**talking incessantly**) may be dangling—that is, that it was not the boy (**he**) but **the girl** who was talking incessantly. If that is so, the writer may not choose the passive verb for the main clause but must use the active verb.

The writers of the sample sentences should consider whether their sentences would be improved by the use of an active verb, as in these revisions:

1 The couple **borrowed** money so that they could pay off all their bills.

2 He **shows** his love for her by accepting her story and by remaining at her side when she is in trouble.

3 From these recurrent images of hard, resistant metals, we **can infer** that she was a mechanical, heartless person.

4 Talking incessantly, the girl **overwhelmed** him.

Paragraphing

One way to regard paragraphing is to view it as a system of punctuating stages of thought presented in units larger than the word and the sentence. Paragraphing is a means of alerting readers to a shift of focus in the development of the main idea of the whole discourse. It marks off for the reader's convenience the individually distinct but related parts of the whole discourse. How paragraphing facilitates reading would be made dramatically evident if a whole discourse were written or printed—as ancient manuscripts once were—in a single, unbroken block.

Like punctuation and mechanics, paragraphing is a feature only of the written language. Some linguists claim that speakers of connected discourse signal their "paragraphs" by pauses and by shifts in the tone of their voice. (The next time you hear a speech being delivered from a written text, see if you can detect when the speaker shifts to another paragraph of his or her text.) But speakers are not conscious—especially in extemporaneous stretches of talk—of paragraphing the stream of sound as writers must be when they are writing their manuscripts.

The typographical device most commonly used to mark off paragraphs is *indentation*. The first line of each new paragraph starts several spaces (usually five or six spaces on the typewriter) from the left-hand margin. Another convention for marking paragraphs is the block system: beginning the first line at the left-hand margin but leaving double or triple spacing between paragraphs. One of the forms of writing that regularly uses the block system is the single-spaced, typewritten business letter.

In this section, only three aspects of the paragraph are treated: unity, coherence, and adequate development. The traditional means of developing the central idea of a paragraph are mentioned in the section on adequate development, but they are not discussed at length. The means of developing paragraphs are fundamentally a concern of invention, which is the province of a rhetoric text rather than of a handbook. However, if writers take care of unity, coherence, and adequate development, they will be attending to the three most persistent and common problems that beset the composition of written paragraphs.

50

Preserve the unity of the paragraph.

Examples of paragraphs lacking unity:

1 The eminence of Samuel Johnson inclines modern scholars to study his thoughts and opinions. His multifarious knowledge intrigued his contemporaries. Although he manifested his interest in the drama by editing Shakespeare, he did not enjoy the theater. He was envious too of his former pupil David Garrick, the greatest actor of the eighteenth century.

2 "The Cradle Song" from the *Songs of Innocence* has internal rhyme. In this poem, the child is quiet and happy. It has a heavenly

Paragraphing

image, and throughout the poem, the mother sheds tears of joy. It has a persona—that is, one who speaks for the poet—who is naive and innocent. The poem "Infant Sorrow" contrasts with "The Cradle Song," and this contrast is very distinct. One can see a screaming and devilish child. The piping is a harsh sound, and the child, who's against restrictions, is looking back and realizing that there is no paradise on earth.

3 Dr. Rockwell let his feelings be known on only one subject: the administration. He felt that the administrative system was outdated. Abolishing grades, giving the student a voice in administration, and revamping the curriculum were three steps he felt should be taken to improve the system. Dr. Rockwell taught in this manner. In class, a mysterious aura surrounded him. He was "hip" to what was going on, but he preferred to hear the members of the class rather than himself. He was quiet and somewhat shy. His eyes caught everything that went on in class. His eyes generated a feeling of understanding.

The principle governing paragraph unity is that a paragraph should develop a single topic or thesis, which is often—but not always—announced in a topic sentence. Every sentence in the paragraph should contribute in some way to the development of that single idea. When writers introduce other ideas into the paragraph, they violate the unity of the paragraph and disorient their readers.

In a sense, all three of the sample paragraphs discuss a single idea or topic: 1 talks about Samuel Johnson; 2 talks about William Blake's poetry; 3 talks about a teacher, Dr. Rockwell. But in another sense, all three paragraphs present a confusing mixture of unrelated ideas.

The first sentence of paragraph 1, which has the air of being a "topic sentence," mentions that modern scholars have turned their attention to a study of Samuel Johnson. Instead of the second sentence going on to develop that idea, it mentions what

Dr. Johnson meant to his contemporaries. The third sentence talks about his attitude toward drama and the theater. The fourth sentence mentions his envy of his former pupil David Garrick. What we have in this paragraph is four topics. A whole paragraph or paper could be devoted to the development of each of these four topics, but here they are packed into a single paragraph.

Paragraph 2, as we have already observed, has a certain unity: each sentence is saying something about a poem by William Blake. Even though this paragraph discusses two different poems by Blake, we can detect some unity in the paragraph if we view it as developing a contrast between two poems by the same author. And, indeed, midway through the paragraph, the writer explicitly announces that the two poems contrast with one another. But even if we were generous enough to concede that much unity to the paragraph, it would be difficult for us to perceive a unifying theme among the many disparate things said about the two poems.

Paragraph 3 also has a certain unity: each sentence in the paragraph is talking about the teacher, Dr. Rockwell. And there is a tight unity in the first three sentences: each of these sentences talks about Dr. Rockwell's attitude toward the administration. But with the fourth sentence of the paragraph, the writer introduces another and unrelated topic: a description of how Dr. Rockwell conducted himself in the classroom. If the writer had broken up this stretch of prose into two paragraphs, each of the two paragraphs would have had its own unity.

Each of the following revisions constitutes one of several ways in which the corresponding sample paragraph might have been unified:

1 The eminence of Samuel Johnson inclines modern scholars to study his thoughts and opinions. A number of recent books and articles

Paragraphing

have dealt with his viewpoints on a variety of his interests. One of those interests was the drama. Curiously, however, although he manifested this interest by writing his own play for the stage and by editing all the plays of Shakespeare, he did not enjoy the theater. Some modern scholars have speculated that he did not enjoy the theater because of his poor eyesight and impaired hearing. Others have speculated that he disliked the theater because he was jealous of his former pupil David Garrick, who very early in his career acquired the reputation of being the greatest actor of his day.

2 William Blake's "The Cradle Song" contrasts distinctly with his poem "Infant Sorrow." Whereas the child in "The Cradle Song" is quiet and happy, the child in "Infant Sorrow" is strident and devilish. Both poems have a persona—that is, one who speaks for the poet— but the persona in "The Cradle Song" is naive and innocent, whereas the persona in the other poem is worldly-wise and guilt-ridden. The rhythms and rhymes in the first poem are smooth and pleasant, but the rhythms and rhymes of the second poem are harsh and discordant. One poem presents an overall mood of contentment; the other presents a mood of disillusionment.

3 Dr. Rockwell let his feelings be known on only one subject: the administration. His estimate of the administrative system of the school was largely negative. He felt, for instance, that the administrative system was outdated. Abolishing grades, giving students a voice in administration, and revamping the curriculum were three steps he felt should be taken to improve the system.

Dr. Rockwell's demeanor in the classroom was remarkable. Although there was a mysterious aura about him, he was always "hip" to what was going on. His eyes caught everything that went on in class, but they generated a feeling of understanding. Even though he was a very learned scholar, this quiet, somewhat shy man preferred to listen to the members of the class rather than himself.

A paragraph will have unity, will have "oneness," if every sentence in it has an obvious bearing on the development of a single topic. When writers sense that they have shifted to the discussion of another topic, they should begin a new paragraph.

51

Compose the paragraph so that it reads coherently.

Examples of incoherent paragraphs:

1 The first stanza of "The Echoing Green" does not correspond with any other poem by Blake. The glory of nature's beauty is presented in vivid details. Emotional intensity is the overall effect of the poem. Blake resents the mechanization which has been brought about by the Industrial Revolution. The rhythm of the verses contributes to the meditative mood.

2 The preceding account illustrates all the frustrations that a beginning golfer experiences. The dominant philosophy is that the golfer who looks the best plays the best. He complicates the game by insisting on perfection the first time he sets foot on the course. More time and money are spent on clothes and equipment than on the most important aspect, skill. Winning is the only goal. Where is the idea of recreation? Try playing without a caddy sometime, and see how much exercise you get.

3 After the program has been written, each line is punched onto a card. The deck of cards is known as the "program source deck." The next step is to load the program compiler into the computer. The compiler is a program written in machine language for a particular computer, which reads the source deck and performs a translation of the program language into machine language. The machine language, in the form of instructions, is punched onto cards. This machine-language deck of cards is known as the "object deck." After the object deck has been punched, the programmer is then able

Paragraphing

to execute his program. The program is run by loading the object deck into the computer. The run of the program marks the end of the second step.

Coherence is that quality which makes it easy for a reader to follow a writer's train of thought from sentence to sentence and from paragraph to paragraph. Coherence facilitates reading because it ensures that the reader will be able to detect the relationship of the parts of a discourse. It also reflects the clear thinking of the writer because it results from the writer's arrangement of ideas in some kind of perceptible order and from the use of those verbal devices that help to stitch thoughts together. In short, as the Latin roots of the word suggest (*co*, "together," + *haerēre*, "to stick"), coherence helps the parts of a discourse "stick together."

Here are some ways in which to achieve coherence in a paragraph (not all of these devices, of course, have to be used in every paragraph):

(a)   Repeat key words from sentence to sentence or use recognizable synonyms for key words.

(b)   Use pronouns for key nouns. (Because a pronoun gets its meaning from the noun to which it refers, it is by its very nature one of those verbal devices that help to stitch sentences together.)

(c)   Use demonstrative adjectives, "pointing words" (**this** statement, **that** plan, **these** developments, **those** disasters).

(d)   Use conjunctive adverbs, "thought-connecting words" **(however, moreover, also, nevertheless, therefore, thus, subsequently, indeed, then, accordingly).**

(e)   Arrange the sequence of sentences in some kind of perceivable order (for instance, a **time order,** as in a narrative of what happened or in an explanation of how to do something;

a **space order,** as in the description of a physical object or a scene; a **logical order,** such as cause to effect, effect to cause, general to particular, particular to general, whole to part, familiar to unfamiliar).

Paragraph 3 above attempts to describe computer programming, a process that most readers would find difficult to follow because it is unfamiliar and complicated. But the process will be doubly difficult for readers if it is not described coherently. What makes this description of computer programming especially difficult to follow is that the writer is doing two things at once in the paragraph: (1) designating the chronological sequence of steps in the process, and (2) defining the technical terms used in the description of the process. It would have been better if the writer had devoted one paragraph to defining such terms as **program source deck, compiler, object deck.** Then the writer could have devoted another paragraph exclusively to the description of the process of "running a program"—first you do this, then you do that, after that you do this, etc. As the paragraph now stands, readers get lost because they are kept bouncing back and forth between definition of the terms and description of the process.

It is more difficult to suggest ways of revising paragraphs 1 and 2; they are so incoherent that it is almost impossible to discover what the principal points were that the writers wanted to put across in them. If we could confer with the writers and ask them what the main idea of their paragraphs was supposed to be, we could then advise them about which of the sentences contributed to the development of that idea (and which sentences had to be dropped because they threatened the unity of the paragraph), about the order of the sentences in the given paragraph, and about the verbal devices that would help to knit the sequence of sentences together.

Paragraphing

Each of the following revisions constitutes one of a number of ways in which the corresponding sample might have been written to give it coherence:

1 It is interesting to note how William Blake achieves the emotional intensity that he does in "The Echoing Green." He achieves that intensity partly by presenting the glory of nature in vivid details that contrast with the dull, gray mechanization of the urban scene that has been produced by the Industrial Revolution. The slow rhythm of the verses also contributes to the emotional intensity by creating a meditative mood. The extraordinary collection of images in the first stanza of the poem also serves to exert a strong emotional effect on the reader.

2 The beginning golfer is often frustrated by the false sense of values that he has been sold. For one thing, he spends more time and money on buying clothes and equipment than on acquiring the most important aspect, skill. Apparently, he has bought the philosophy that the golfer who looks the best plays the best. Moreover, because he has bought the philosophy that winning is the only goal, he has lost sight of the goal of recreation. He insists on perfection the first time he sets foot on the course instead of being satisfied with the fun and exercise he gets from playing a round of eighteen holes.

3 Before you can understand the process of "running a program," you need some definitions of technical terms. After the program discussed in the previous paragraph has been written, each line of that program is punched onto an IBM card. The collection of these cards is known as the "program source deck." Another set of cards is known as the "compiler." The compiler "reads" the source deck and translates it into machine language. The machine-language deck of cards that results from the operation of the compiler is known as the "object deck."

The first step in the process is to put the program source deck into the computer. Then in order to translate the program language of the source deck into machine language, the compiler set must be inserted. Following that step, the object deck, with its instructions written out in machine language, is put into the computer. Now the program is ready to be "run" through the computer.

Coherence is a difficult writing skill to master, but until writers acquire at least a measure of that skill, they will continue to be frustrated in their efforts to communicate with others on paper. They must learn how to compose paragraphs so that the sequence of thoughts flows smoothly, easily, and logically from sentence to sentence. They must provide those bridges or links that will allow the reader to pass from sentence to sentence without being puzzled about the relationship of what is said in one sentence to what is said in the next sentence.

Note how a skillful writer like Thomas Babington Macaulay stitches sentences together by repeating key words and by using pronouns, conjunctive words, and parallel structures:

It will be seen that we do not consider Bacon's ingenious analysis of the inductive method as a very useful performance. Bacon was not, as we have already said, the inventor of the inductive method. He was not even the person who first analyzed the inductive method correctly, though he undoubtedly analyzed it more minutely than any who preceded him. He was not the person who first showed that by the inductive method alone new truth could be discovered. But he was the person who first turned the minds of speculative men, long occupied in verbal disputes, to the discovery of new and useful truth; and by doing so, he at once gave to the inductive method an importance and dignity which had never belonged to it. He was not the maker of that road; he was not the discoverer of that road; he was not the person who first surveyed and mapped that road. But he was the person who first called the public attention to an inexhaustible mine of wealth, which had been utterly neglected and which was accessible by that road alone. By doing so, he caused that road, which had previously been trodden only by peasants and higglers, to be frequented by a higher class of travellers.

Paragraphing

52

Paragraphs should be adequately developed.

Examples of inadequately developed paragraphs:

1 The government has resorted to many methods of preventing tax frauds. Most of these methods have proved ineffective so far.

2 The young people now growing up in this drug-oriented atmosphere should be made aware of the disadvantages of their indulging in drugs, just as the young people of the previous generation were cautioned about the disadvantages of their engaging in premarital sex. In both cases, responsibility for one's actions is the chief lesson to be taught.

3 Before we seek answers to those questions, however, we should settle on a definition of the term *illiteracy*. For most people, *illiteracy* signifies the inability to read and write.

Generally, one- and two-sentence paragraphs are not justifiable, except for purposes of emphasis, transition, or dialogue.

Note that this last sentence is also a paragraph, justifiable as such on the grounds that the writer wanted to give special emphasis to a principle by setting it aside in a paragraph by itself. Separate paragraphing for emphasis is a graphic device comparable to underlining a word or a phrase in a sentence for emphasis. Set aside in a paragraph by itself, an important idea achieves a prominence that would be missed if the idea were merged with other ideas in the same paragraph.

A one- or two-sentence paragraph can also be used to mark or signal a transition from one major division of a discourse to the next major division. These transitional paragraphs facilitate reading because they orient readers, reminding them of what has been discussed and alerting them to what is going to be discussed. Such paragraphs are like signposts marking the major stages of a journey. Note how the following two-sentence transitional paragraph looks backward to what has been discussed and forward to what will be discussed:

> After presenting his introduction to *Songs of Experience*, William Blake apparently feels that his readers have been sufficiently warned about their earthly predicament. Let us see now how he uses the poems in *Songs of Experience* to illustrate what the people might do to solve their problems.

One of the conventions of printing is that in representing dialogue in a story, we should begin a new paragraph every time the speaker changes. A paragraph of dialogue can be one sentence long or ten sentences long (any number of sentences, in fact). A paragraph of dialogue may also consist of only a phrase or a single word. Note the paragraphing of the following stretch of dialogue:

> "Look at that cloudless blue sky," Melvin said. "There doesn't seem to be any bottom to that blue. It's beautiful, isn't it?"
>
> "Yup," Hank muttered.
>
> "Remember yesterday?"
>
> "Yup."
>
> "I thought it would never stop raining."
>
> "Me too."

Once an exchange like that gets going, the author can dispense with the identifying tags, because each separate paragraph will mark the shift in speaker.

But except for the purposes of emphasis, transition, or dialogue, a one- or a two-sentence paragraph can rarely be justified. One sentence is hardly enough to qualify as both the topic sentence and the development of the idea posed by that topic. Many times even three- and four-sentence paragraphs are not adequately developed. You will frequently see one-, two-, and

Paragraphing

sometimes three-sentence paragraphs in a newspaper, but newspapers arbitrarily break up paragraphs into small units merely to facilitate reading. In the narrow columns of a newspaper, a five- or six-sentence paragraph would look forbiddingly dense. So the short paragraph is a convention used by all newspapers.

Judgment about whether a paragraph is adequately developed is, of course, a relative matter. Because some ideas need more development than others, no one can say how many sentences a paragraph needs to be adequately developed. Each paragraph must be judged on its own terms and in the context in which it appears. If a paragraph has a topic sentence, for instance, that sentence can dictate how long the paragraph needs to be. What was done in the previous paragraph and what will be done in the paragraph that follows may dictate how long the middle paragraph needs to be.

The sample paragraphs have all been taken out of context, but even so, we can sense the inadequate development of these skimpy paragraphs. Paragraph **1**, for instance, raises some expectations that are not satisfied. The first sentence mentions **many methods**, and we expect that the next sentence will go on to specify at least one of those many methods. Instead, the writer changes the subject: we are now told that these methods (unspecified) have proved ineffective. First of all, the writer has to decide whether he or she wants this paragraph to specify the many methods that the government has used to prevent tax frauds or whether it is preferable to show how or why the methods proved ineffective. Having settled on the topic of the paragraph, the writer can then make some decisions about how to develop the paragraph and how much to develop it.

Even if paragraph **2** were a summary paragraph that followed a paragraph (or several paragraphs) in which the writer had discussed the disadvantages of indulging in drugs, the reader could reasonably expect the writer to say something more about the notion presented in the second sentence. What kind of legal or moral responsibilities do addicts have to themselves? What kind of responsibilities do they have to their family and to society in general? Once addicts have been "hooked," can they still be held responsible for their actions? What are the consequences, for themselves and for society, of their refusing to be responsible for their actions? These questions suggest ways in which the writer might have expanded the thinly developed paragraph.

A reader may feel that paragraph 3 is developed as much as it needs to be. The writer has suggested the need for a definition of the term **illiteracy** and in the next sentence has provided a definition of the term. But even lacking the context of both the paragraph that went before and the paragraph that came after this one, we can judge this paragraph to be inadequately developed. The mere fact that the writer felt the need to seek a definition of a principal term before going on with the discussion indicates that the writer recognized the slipperiness of the term. The phrase that begins the second sentence, **For most people,** suggests that regardless of the common meaning of **illiteracy** (an inability to read and write), the term has other meanings for other people. What the reader expects to get in this paragraph and doesn't get is an exposition of the word's complex meanings. Refining the definition of the word **illiteracy** is one of the ways of expanding the paragraph.

The first step in developing a paragraph is to consider its central idea—whether that is expressed in a topic sentence or merely implied—and determine what that idea commits one to do. It sometimes helps to ask oneself questions like those that were asked above about the second sample paragraph. If such questioning establishes what one is committed to do in a para-

Paragraphing

graph, one can then make a choice of the appropriate means of developing the paragraph. Here is a list of the common ways in which writers develop their paragraphs:

(a)   **They present examples or illustrations of what they are discussing.**

(b)   **They cite data—facts, statistics, evidence, details, precedents—that corroborate or confirm what they are discussing.**

(c)   **They quote, paraphrase, or summarize the testimony of others about what they are discussing.**

(d)   **They relate an anecdote or event that has some bearing on what they are discussing.**

(e)   **They define terms connected with what they are discussing.**

(f)   **They compare or contrast what they are discussing with something else—usually something familiar to the readers—and point out similarities or differences.**

(g)   **They explore the causes or reasons for the phenomenon or situation they are discussing.**

(h)   **They point out the effects or consequences of the phenomenon or situation they are discussing.**

(i)   **They explain how something operates.**

(j)   **They describe the person, place, or thing they are discussing.**

Using one or other of these means of development, we could expand the inadequately developed sample paragraphs. Each of the following revisions constitutes one way in which the corresponding sample paragraph might have been expanded:

1 Most of the methods that the government has resorted to in order to prevent tax frauds have proved ineffective. For instance, the government tried the system of requiring restaurant owners to report

not only the salaries of waiters but also the amount of their daily tips. The waiters, of course, circumvented that system by never reporting the correct total of their tips. Cabdrivers, bellhops, doormen, and others whose chief source of income is tips are a problem too. The government tried setting a standard tip-per-transaction, but these employees rarely reported the correct number of customers they had served, and there was no way that the government could reliably check the figures that were reported. Those who are self-employed constitute the major problem for the Internal Revenue Service. All efforts to get the self-employed to keep and to report accurate or honest records of business transactions have proven futile. It seems that if you are determined enough and smart enough you can evade even the most ingenious efforts of the IRS to make you pay all the taxes that you should pay.
(*expanded by giving examples*)

2 Young people who develop an addiction to drugs should be made aware of their responsibilities for their actions. They must be taught that their insatiable appetite for drugs has consequences not only for themselves but also for family, friends, and society. Parents are the ones who are hurt the most by a son or daughter who gets hooked on drugs. They suffer deeply when they see someone they love become a slave to drugs; and they also feel ashamed and guilt-ridden for their child's addiction. Friends too suffer anguish and humiliation; but they suffer most from the loss of the companionship of a former friend. The effects on society are too numerous to specify completely, but they include the dangers from an addict's resort to violent crimes, the cost of maintaining special police forces, and the loss of a valuable contributing member to the community. Drug addicts don't just ruin themselves; they affect the lives of dozens of other people.
(*expanded by pointing out the effects or consequences of a situation*)

3 Before we seek answers to those questions, however, we should settle on a definition of the term *illiteracy*. For most people, *illiteracy* signifies a person's inability to read and write. But that general defi-

Paragraphing

nition does not reveal the wide range of disabilities covered by the term. There are those who cannot read or write anything in their native language. Others can read minimally, but they cannot write anything—not even their own name. A large number of people have minimal skills in reading and writing, but they cannot apply those skills to some of the ordinary tasks of day-to-day living—e.g. they cannot make sense of the written instructions on a can of weed-killer or fill out an application form. Such people are sometimes referred to as being "functionally illiterate." So whenever we discuss the problem of illiteracy with others, we should make sure what degree of disability people have in mind when they use the term *illiteracy*.

(*expanded by defining or explaining a key term*)

Punctuation

Graphic punctuation, which is the only kind dealt with in this section, is a feature of the written language exclusively. For the written language, it performs the kinds of functions that intonation (pitch, stress, pause, and juncture) performs for the spoken language. Punctuation and intonation can be considered as part of the grammar of a language because they join with other grammatical devices (word order, inflections, and function words) to help convey meaning. If writers would regard punctuation as an integral—and often indispensable—part of the expressive system of a language, they might cease to think of it as just another nuisance imposed on them by editors and English teachers.

In *Structural Essentials of English* (New York: Harcourt Brace Jovanovich, 1956), Harold Whitehall has neatly summarized the four main functions of graphic punctuation:

☐ **For LINKING parts of sentences and words.**
semicolon **;**
colon **:**
dash **▬**
hyphen (for words only) **▬**

Punctuation

☐ **For SEPARATING sentences and parts of sentences.**

period **.**

question mark **?**

exclamation point **!**

comma **,**

☐ **For ENCLOSING parts of sentences.**

pair of commas **, ... ,**

pair of dashes **▬ ... ▬**

pair of parentheses **(...)**

pair of brackets **[...]**

pair of quotation marks **" ..."**

☐ **For INDICATING omissions.**

apostrophe (e.g. **don't, we'll, it's, we've**)

period (e.g. abbreviations, **Mrs., U.S., A. H. Robinson**)

dash (e.g. **John R–, D–n!**)

triple periods (**. . .** to indicate omitted words in a quotation)

Punctuation is strictly a convention. There is no reason in the nature of things why the mark **?** should be used in English to indicate a question. The Greek language, for instance, uses **;** (what we call a semicolon) to mark questions. Nor is there any reason in the nature of things why the single comma should be a separating device rather than a linking device. It is usage that has established the distinctive functions of the various marks of punctuation. And although styles of punctuation have changed somewhat from century to century and even from country to country, the conventions of punctuation set forth in the following section are the prevailing conventions in the United States in the last quarter of the twentieth century. Although publishers of newspapers, magazines, and books often have style manuals that prescribe, for their own editors and writers, a style of punctuation that may differ in some particulars from the prevailing conventions, writers who observe the conventions of punctuation set forth in this section can rest assured that they are following the predominant system in the United States.

60

Put a comma in front of the coordinating conjunction that joins the independent clauses of a compound sentence.

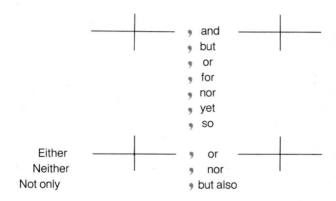

Examples of compound sentences that need a comma:

1 He disliked this kind of cruel humor yet he continued to tease her unmercifully.

Punctuation

2 Alice's embarrassment amused Julian so he deliberately pursued the conversation with the Dirty Old Man across the aisle.

3 He returned the book for his mother refused to pay any more fines.

4 The decision about whether to attend college should be left entirely to the children and their parents should make every effort to reconcile themselves to the decision.

5 It was snowing outside and in the building Kazuko felt safe.

6 Either the senators will reject the proposal or they will modify it in such a way as to make it innocuous.

This convention of the comma comes into play only in compound sentences (sentences composed of two or more independent clauses) or in compound-complex sentences (sentences composed of two or more independent clauses and at least one dependent clause). According to **62**, pairs of words, phrases, or clauses (except independent clauses) joined by one of the coordinating conjunctions should *not* be separated with a comma.

This practice of using a comma probably developed because in many compounded sentences, the absence of the comma could lead to an initial misreading of the sentence. In sentence **1**, for instance, it would be quite natural for us to read **for** as a preposition and consequently to read the sentence this way: **He returned the book for his mother**. . . . But when we came to the verb **refused**, we would realize that we had misread the syntax of the sentence, and we would have to back up and reread the sentence. Likewise, in sentence **4**, we tend to read the sentence in this way: . . . **should be left entirely to the children and their parents**. . . . But when we read on, we realize that the absence of a comma before the conjunction **and** has trapped us into a misreading of the syntax of the sentence. A comma placed before the coordinating conjunction that joins the independent clauses of a compound sentence will prevent such misreadings.

Some handbooks authorize you to omit this separating comma under certain conditions. However, if you *invariably* insert a comma before the coordinating conjunction that joins the independent clauses, you never have to pause to consider whether those conditions are present, and you can be confident that your sentence will always be read correctly the first time. So the safest practice is *always* to insert the comma before the coordinating conjunction or before the second of the correlative conjunctions (**either . . . or; neither . . . nor; not only . . . but also**) that join the main clauses of a compound or compound-complex sentence.

Here are the sample sentences with the comma inserted in the proper place:

1 He disliked this kind of cruel humor, yet he continued to tease her unmercifully.

2 Alice's embarrassment amused Julian, so he deliberately pursued the conversation with the Dirty Old Man across the aisle.

3 He returned the book, for his mother refused to pay any more fines.

4 The decision about whether to attend college should be left entirely to the children, and their parents should make every effort to reconcile themselves to the decision.

5 It was snowing outside, and in the building Kazuko felt safe.

6 Either the senators will reject the proposal, or they will modify it in such a way as to make it innocuous.

61

Introductory words, phrases, or clauses should be separated from the main (independent) clause by a comma.

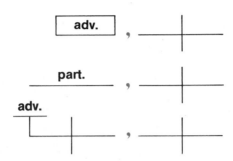

Examples of introductory words, phrases, and clauses that need a comma:

1 Underneath the papers were scorched.
(*introductory word*)

2 I tiptoed into the house. Inside the front room looked as though it had been recently painted by a group of three-year-olds.
(*introductory word*)

3 In addition to the logical errors Doris had made several miscalculations in addition and subtraction.
(*introductory prepositional phrase*)

4 As we went by the church revealed all of its redbrick Georgian elegance.
(*introductory adverbial clause*)

5 After hurriedly gathering the crowd decided to rush the gates.
(*introductory verbal phrase*)

6 Although she vehemently protested the violence was not as destructive as he predicted it would be.
(*introductory adverbial clause*)

The reason this convention developed is that the comma facilitates the reading of the sentence and often prevents an initial misreading. Without the "protective" comma, the syntax of the six sample sentences above would probably be misread on the first reading. The likelihood is that you read the sample sentences this way the first time:

1 **Underneath the papers ...**
2 **Inside the front room ...**
3 **In addition to the logical errors [that] Doris had made ...**
4 **As we went by the church ...**
5 **After hurriedly gathering the crowd ...**
6 **Although she vehemently protested the violence ...**

The insertion of a comma after each of these introductory elements would have prevented that kind of misreading.

Even in those instances, however, where there is little or no chance of an initial misreading, the insertion of a comma after the introductory word, phrase, or clause will facilitate the reading of the sentence. If you read the following sentences twice, the first time without the comma, the second time with the comma after the introductory word, phrase, or clause, you will discover that it is easier to read and understand the sentences that have a comma after the introductory element:

Besides the crowd wasn't impressed by his flaming oratory.

Having failed to impress the crowd with his flaming oratory he tried another tactic.

After he saw that his flaming oratory had not impressed the crowd he tried another tactic.

Punctuation

Here now are the sample sentences with a comma inserted after the introductory word, phrase, or clause:

1 Underneath **,** the papers were scorched.
2 I tiptoed into the house. Inside **,** the front room looked as though it had been recently painted by a group of three-year-olds.
3 In addition to the logical errors **,** Doris had made several miscalculations in addition and substraction.
4 As we went by **,** the church revealed all of its redbrick Georgian elegance.
5 After hurriedly gathering **,** the crowd decided to rush the gates.
6 Although she vehemently protested **,** the violence was not as destructive as he predicted it would be.

If writers *always* insert a comma after an introductory word, phrase, or clause, they will not have to consider each time whether it would be safe to omit the comma, and they can be confident that their sentence will not be misread.

62

Pairs of words, phrases, or dependent clauses joined by one of the coordinating conjunctions should not be separated with a comma.

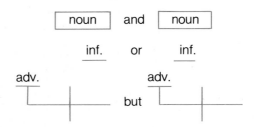

Examples of pairs incorrectly separated by a comma;

1 The mother, and the father appeared in court, and testified about their son's activities.
2 There was nothing they could do to prevent the gas attack, or to protect themselves against the gas once it had been released.
3 The men who are able to work, but who are not willing to work will not be eligible to receive monthly welfare checks.
4 Marian was happiest when she was free of her parents' scrutiny, or while she was working in her garden.

The principle behind this convention is that what has been joined by one means (the coordinating conjunction) should not then be separated by another means (the comma, a separating device). The function of the coordinating conjunction is to join units of equal rank (e.g. nouns with nouns, verbs with verbs, prepositional phrases with prepositional phrases, adjective clauses with adjective clauses). Once pairs of coordinate units have been joined by the conjunction, it makes no sense to separate them with a comma—as has been done in all the sample sentences above.

A pair of *independent* clauses is not covered by this rule. According to **60**, a comma should be inserted before the coordinating conjunction, because in this structure the omission of the comma could lead—and often does lead—to an initial misreading of the sentence. But there are almost no instances where the use of a comma would prevent the misreading of pairs of words, phrases, or dependent clauses joined by a coordinating conjunction. As a matter of fact, sentence **1** is harder to read because of the comma that separates the two nouns of the subject (**mother** and **father**) and the two verbs of the predicate (**appeared** and **testified**). The commas used in that sentence only confuse the reader.

Punctuation

An exception to this convention occurs in the case of suspended structures, as in the following sentence:

> This account of an author's struggles with, and her anxieties about, her writing fascinated me.

The phrases **struggles with** and **anxieties about** are called *suspended structures* because they are left "hanging" until the noun phrase **her writing**, which completes them grammatically, occurs. If this sentence could have been written

> This account of an author's struggles and anxieties about her writing fascinated me.

there would not be, according to **62**, a comma in front of the **and** that joins the pair of nouns **struggles** and **anxieties**. Here the preposition **about** fits idiomatically with **anxieties** but does not fit idiomatically with **struggles**. In such cases, writers are faced with a choice. Either they can complete both structures and write

> This account of an author's struggles with her writing and her anxieties about her writing fascinated me.

Or, if they prefer to avoid the repetition of **her writing**, they can choose to use suspended structures, and they can alert the reader to the structures by putting a comma after **with** and after **about**:

> This account of an author's struggles with, and anxieties about, her writing fascinated me.

In this case, inserting a comma before the conjunction **and**, which joins the two phrases, makes it easier for us to read the sentence.

With this exception, the joining device (the conjunction) and the separating device (the comma) should not work against one another.

Here are the sample sentences with the superfluous commas deleted:

1 The **mother** and the **father appeared** in court and **testified** about their son's activities.
   (*two nouns and two verbs joined by **and***)

2 There was nothing they could do **to prevent the gas attack** or **to protect themselves** against the gas once it had been released.
   (*two infinitive phrases joined by **or***)

3 The men **who are able to work** but **who are not willing to work** will not be eligible to receive monthly welfare checks.
   (*two adjective clauses joined by **but***)

4 Marian was happiest **when she was free of her parents' scrutiny** or **while she was working in her garden**.
   (*two adverb clauses joined by **or***)

63

Use a comma to separate a series of coordinate words, phrases, or clauses.

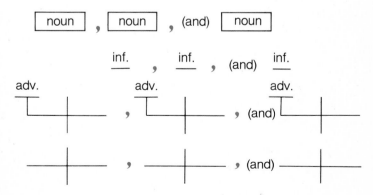

Punctuation

*(The parentheses around **and** in the diagrams above indicate that the coordinating conjunction between the last two members of a series may sometimes be dispensed with. For instance, the phrasing **The tall, robust, gray-haired soldier rose to speak** is stylistically preferable to **The tall, robust, and gray-haired soldier rose to speak**.)*

Examples of series lacking one or more commas:

1 Could he cope with the challenges posed by war, poverty, pollution and crime?
   (*a series of nouns*)

2 He would have to terminate the war, alleviate the plight of the poor, arrest the contamination of the environment and hobble the criminal.
   (*series of infinitive phrases, with* **to** *understood in the last three members of the series*)

3 If she is willing to work if she is resourceful enough to formulate sensible policies if she subordinates her own interests to the interests of the community, she can rescue the nation from the despair that now prevails.
   (*series of adverb clauses*)

4 She wanted to save the nation, she knew she could save it and eventually she did save it.
   (*series of independent clauses*)

Whereas the convention stated in **62** says that *pairs* of coordinate words, phrases, or clauses should not be separated with a comma, the convention governing a *series* of coordinate words, phrases, and clauses says that these units should be separated with commas. (*A series is to be understood as a sequence of three or more coordinate units.*) Built on the principle of parallelism (see **27**), the series always involves words, phrases, or clauses of a similar kind. So a series should never couple nouns with adjectives, prepositional phrases with infinitive phrases, adjective clauses with adverb clauses, etc.

The convention that will be recommended here follows this formula:

a, b, and c.

Another acceptable formula for the series is

a, b and c

where no comma is used between the last two members of the series when they are joined by a coordinating conjunction. The formula **a, b, and c** is adopted here because the alternative formula (**a, b and c**) sometimes leads to ambiguity. Consider the following example, which uses the **a, b and c** formula:

> Please send me a gross each of the red, green, blue, orange and black ties.

The shipping clerk who received that order might wonder whether five gross of ties (**red, green, blue, orange, black**) were being ordered or only four gross (**red, green, blue, orange-and-black**). If five gross were being ordered, a comma after **orange** would specify the order unambiguously; if four gross were being ordered, hyphens should have been used to signify the combination of colors.

A more common instance of the ambiguity that is sometimes created by the use of the **a, b and c** formula is the following:

> He appealed to the administrators, the deans and the chairpersons.

In this sentence, it is not clear whether he appealed to three different groups (**administrators, deans, chairpersons**)—a meaning that would have been clearly indicated by the **a, b, and c** formula—or to only one group, **administrators,** who are then specified in the two appositives **deans** and **chairpersons**.

Punctuation

Since there is never any chance of ambiguity if you use the **a, b, and c** formula, you would be well advised to adopt this option for punctuating a series.

Here are the sample sentences revised to make them conform to the **a, b, and c** formula:

1 Could he cope with the challenges posed by war, poverty, pollution, and crime?

2 He would have to terminate the war, alleviate the plight of the poor, arrest the contamination of the environment, and hobble the criminal.

3 If she is willing to work, if she is resourceful enough to formulate sensible policies, if she subordinates her own interests to the interests of the community, she can rescue the nation from the despair that now prevails.

4 She wanted to save the nation, she knew she could save it, and eventually she did save it.

64

Nonrestrictive adjective clauses should be enclosed with a pair of commas.

Examples of nonrestrictive adjective clauses that should be enclosed with commas:

1 My oldest brother   was hurt in an accident last week.

2 The shopkeeper caters only to American tourists **who usually have enough money to buy what they want** and to aristocratic families.

3 Norman Mailer's book **which most reviewers considered juvenile in its pronouncements** was severely panned by feminist-movement groups.

4 The townspeople threaten the strangers **who are looking at the young girl.**

A nonrestrictive adjective clause is one that supplies information about the noun that it modifies but information that is not needed to identify or specify the particular person, place, or thing that is being talked about. (The four **that** clauses in this last sentence, for instance, are *restrictive* adjective clauses—clauses that supply *necessary* identifying or specifying information about the nouns that they modify.)

In sentence **1**, the adjective clause **who is a chemist** supplies additional information about **my oldest brother**, but this information is not needed to identify which of the brothers was hurt in the accident, because the adjective **oldest** sufficiently identifies the brother being talked about.

One test to determine whether an adjective clause is nonrestrictive is to read the sentence without it, and if the particular person, place, or thing being talked about is sufficiently identified by what is left, the adjective clause can be considered nonrestrictive—and, according to the convention, should be marked off with enclosing commas. If, for instance, you were to drop the adjective clause from sentence **1** and say **My oldest brother was hurt in an accident last week**, your readers would not have to ask, ''Which one of your brothers was hurt?'' The brother that was hurt is specified by the adjective **oldest**, since there can be only one oldest brother. The clause **who is a chemist** merely supplies some additional but nonessential information about the oldest brother.

Punctuation

Another test to determine whether an adjective clause is nonrestrictive is the *intonation* test. Read these two written versions of sentence **2** aloud:

> He caters to American tourists, who have enough money to buy what they want, and to aristocratic families.
>
> He caters to American tourists who have enough money to buy what they want and to aristocratic families.

In reading the first sentence aloud, native speakers of the language would pause briefly after the words **tourists** and **want** (that is, in the places where the commas are) and would lower the pitch of their voices slightly in enunciating the clause **who have enough money to buy what they want**. In reading the second sentence aloud, native speakers would read right through without a pause and would not lower the pitch of their voices in reading the adjective clause.

In writing, it makes a *significant* difference whether the adjective clause in a sentence is marked off with commas or not. *With* the enclosing commas, sentence **2**, for instance, means this: He caters to American tourists (who, incidentally, usually have enough money to buy what they want) and to aristocratic families. *Without* the enclosing commas, the sentence means this: He caters only to those American tourists who have enough money to buy what they want (he doesn't cater to any American tourists who don't have enough money to buy) and to aristocratic families. Those two meanings are quite different from one another, and for that reason, it is extremely important, in a written text, whether or not the adjective clause is marked off with commas.

Likewise, it is important whether or not the adjective clause in sentence **4** is marked off with commas. Without the comma before the **who** clause, the sentence means that the townspeople threaten only those strangers who are looking at the young

116

girl (with the implication that some are not looking at her). But it was clear from the context in which that sentence occurred that the writer meant to say that the townspeople threatened *all* the strangers—all of whom were looking lasciviously at the young girl. The way the writer should have signaled this latter meaning was to put a comma before the **who** clause, thus indicating that this adjective clause was to be read as a nonrestrictive clause.

There are some instances in which the adjective clause is almost invariably nonrestrictive:

(a)   Where the antecedent is a **proper noun,** the adjective clause is usually nonrestrictive:

Martin Chuzzlewit, who is a character in Dicken's novel, . . .

New York City, which has the largest urban population in the United States, . . .

The College of William and Mary, which was founded in 1693, . . .

(b)   Where, in the nature of things, there could be **only one such** person, place, or thing, the adjective clause is usually nonrestrictive:

My mother, who is now forty-six years old, . . .

Their birthplace, which is Jamestown, . . .

His fingerprints, which are on file in Washington, . . .

(c)   Where the identity of the antecedent has been clearly established by the **previous context,** the adjective clause is usually nonrestrictive:

My brother, who has hazel eyes, . . . (where it is clear from the context that you have only one brother)

The book, which never made the bestseller list, . . . (where the previous sentence has identified the particular book being talked about)

Such revolutions, which never enlist the sympathies of the majority of the people, . . . (where the kinds of revolutions being talked about have been specified in the previous sentences or paragraphs)

Punctuation

Which is the usual relative pronoun that introduces nonrestrictive adjective clauses. **That** is the more common relative pronoun used in restrictive adjective clauses. **Who** (or its inflected forms **whose** and **whom**) is the usual relative pronoun when the antecedent is a person; **that,** however, may also be used when the antecedent is a person and the clause is restrictive: either "the men whom I admire" or "the men that I admire."

Here are revisions of the sample sentences with the nonrestrictive adjective clauses properly marked off with enclosing commas. (Incidentally, sentence 4 does not have the second of the pair of enclosing commas because the adjective clause occurs at the end of the sentence rather than, as the others do, somewhere in the middle of the sentence.)

1 My oldest brother, who is a chemist, was hurt in an accident last week.

2 The shopkeeper caters only to American tourists, who usually have enough money to buy what they want, and to aristocratic families.

3 Norman Mailer's book, which most reviewers considered juvenile in its pronouncements, was severely panned by feminist-movement groups.

4 The townspeople threaten the strangers, who are looking at the young girl.

65

Restrictive adjective clauses should not be marked off with a pair of commas.

(no comma)   (no comma)

Examples of adjective clauses that should not be marked off with a pair of commas:

1 Middle-aged people **,** who have slow reflexes **,** should be denied a driver's license.

2 The poem is about a girl **,** who has been in Vietnam and has rejoined her family.

3 All streets, alleys, and thoroughfares **,** that are in the public domain **,** should be maintained by the city.

A restrictive adjective clause is one that identifies or specifies the particular person, place, or thing being talked about. It "restricts" the noun that it modifies; it "defines"—that is, "draws boundaries around"—the noun being talked about. Nonrestrictive clauses, as we saw in **64**, give *additional* information about the nouns that they modify, but they do not serve to *identify* or *specify* the noun that they modify.

In sentence **1**, the adjective clause **who have slow reflexes** is restrictive because it identifies, defines, designates, specifies *which* middle-aged people should be denied a driver's license. The writer of that sentence did not intend to say that *all* middle-aged people should be denied a driver's license, but with the commas enclosing the adjective clause, the sentence does suggest that all of them should not be allowed to drive. The

Punctuation

writer meant to say that only those middle-aged people who have slow reflexes should be denied a driver's license. Leaving out the enclosing commas will make the sentence say what the writer intended to say.

The commas in sentences **2** and **3** should also be omitted. The **who** clause in sentence **2** "restricts" the kind of girl that the poem is about. If the commas enclosing the **that** clause in sentence **3** are omitted, the sentence will say what the writer obviously intended to say: that the city is responsible for maintaining only those streets, alleys, and thoroughfares that are in the public domain.

If you were speaking those three sentences, your voice would do what the presence or the absence of the commas does. If the commas are left out—as they should be—your voice would join the adjective clause to the noun or nouns that it modifies by running on without a pause after the nouns. With the commas, your voice would pause momentarily at those junctures, and a different meaning would be conveyed.

According to the convention, restrictive adjective clauses modifying nonhuman nouns should be introduced with the relative pronoun **that** rather than with **which**:

Governments, which are instituted to protect the rights of men, should be responsive to the will of the people.
(*nonrestrictive*)

Governments that want to remain in favor with their constituents must be responsive to the will of the people.
(*restrictive*)

Here is another distinctive fact about the phrasing of restrictive and nonrestrictive clauses: the relative pronoun may sometimes be omitted in restrictive clauses, but it may never be omitted in nonrestrictive clauses. Note that it is impossible in English to drop the relative pronouns **who** and **whom** from the following nonrestrictive clauses:

John, who is my dearest friend, won't drink with me.

John, whom I love dearly, hardly notices me.

(In the first sentence, however, the clause **who is my dearest friend** could be reduced to an appositive phrase: **John, *my dearest friend*, won't drink with me**.)

In restrictive adjective clauses, we sometimes have the option of using or not using the relative pronoun:

The one whom I love dearly hardly notices me.
(*with the relative pronoun*)

The one that I love dearly hardly notices me.
(*with the relative pronoun*)

The one I love dearly hardly notices me.
(*without the relative pronoun*)

In restrictive adjective clauses like these, where the relative pronoun serves as the object of the verb of the adjective clause, the relative pronoun may be omitted. The relative pronoun in restrictive clauses may also be omitted if it serves as the object of a preposition in the adjective clause: "The man I gave the wallet to disappeared" (here the understood *whom* or *that* serves as the object of the preposition **to**). However, the relative pronoun may *not* be omitted when it serves as the subject of the restrictive adjective clause:

He who exalts himself shall be humbled.
(***who** cannot be omitted*)

The money that was set aside for scholarships was squandered on roads.
(***that** cannot be omitted*)

Here are the sample sentences with the separating commas deleted:

1 Middle-aged people who have slow reflexes should be denied a driver's license.

2 The poem is about a girl who has been in Vietnam and has rejoined her family.

3 All streets, alleys, and thoroughfares that are in the public domain should be maintained by the city.

66

If the independent clauses of a compound sentence are not joined by one of the coordinating conjunctions, they should be joined by a semicolon.

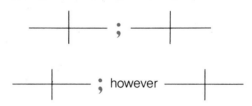

Examples of compound sentences that should be joined by a semicolon:

1 This refutation is based on an appeal to reason however, one must remember that an emotional appeal can also move people to reject an argument.

2 All the students spontaneously supported the team, they wanted to show their loyalty, even though they were disappointed with the outcome of the game.

3 She loved her father, in fact, she practically worshiped him.

The coordinating conjunctions are **and, but, or, nor, for, yet, so.** In the absence of one of those words, the independent clauses of a compound sentence should be spliced together with a punctuation device: the semicolon.

66 Semicolon, Compound Sentence

Words and phrases like **however, therefore, then, indeed, nevertheless, consequently, thus, moreover, furthermore, in fact, on the other hand, on the contrary** are not coordinating conjunctions; they are called *conjunctive adverbs*. Conjunctive adverbs provide logical links between sentences and between parts of sentences, but they do not function as grammatical splicers. Unlike coordinating conjunctions, which must always be placed *between* the two elements they join, conjunctive adverbs enjoy some freedom of movement in the sentence.

In sentence **1**, the word **however** is placed between the two independent clauses, but evidence that this conjunctive adverb is not serving as the grammatical splicer of the two clauses is provided by the fact that **however** can be shifted to another position in the sentence: **This refutation is based on an appeal to reason; one must remember, however, that an emotional appeal can also move people to reject an argument.** The coordinating conjunction **but**, on the other hand, which is equivalent in meaning to **however**, could occupy no other position in the sentence than *between* the end of the first clause (after the word **reason**) and the beginning of the next clause (before the word **one**).

Nor can the independent clauses of a compound sentence be joined by a comma, because the comma is a separating device, not a joining device. Compound sentences so punctuated—like sentence **2**—are called **comma splices** (see **30**). As indicated in **60**, if a compound sentence is joined by one of the coordinating conjunctions, a comma should be put in front of the conjunction to mark off the end of one independent clause and the beginning of the next independent clause. But whenever a coordinating conjunction is not present to join the independent clauses, a semicolon must be used to join them. The semicolon serves both to mark the division between the two clauses and to join them.

Punctuation

Sometimes it is advisable to use both a semicolon and a coordinating conjunction to join the independent clauses of a compound sentence. When the clauses are unusually long and have commas within them, a semicolon placed before the coordinating conjunction helps to demarcate the end of one clause and the beginning of the next one, as in this example:

> Struggling to salvage what was left of the semester, he pleaded with his English teacher, who was notoriously softhearted, to grant him an extension of time on his written assignments, quizzes, and class reports **;** **but** he forgot that, even with the best of intentions, he had only so many hours every day when he could study and only a limited reserve of energy.

The coordinating conjunction **but** serves to join the two main clauses of the compound sentence, but the use of the semicolon in addition to the conjunction makes it easier to read the sentence.

Here are the sample sentences with the splicing semicolon inserted in the proper place:

1 This refutation is based on an appeal to reason**;** however, one must remember that an emotional appeal can also move people to reject an argument.

2 All the students spontaneously supported the team**;** they wanted to show their loyalty, even though they were disappointed with the outcome of the game.

3 She loved her father**;** in fact, she practically worshiped him.

67

Whenever you use a semicolon, be sure that you have an independent clause on both sides of the semicolon.

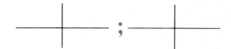

Examples of failure to observe this convention:

1 She played the guitar expertly; although she couldn't read a note of music.

2 Americans spend far too many hours as spectators of sports instead of as participants in them; watching meaningless drivel on television instead of spending that time reading a book.

3 The two series of poems also differ in style; the *Songs of Experience* being more vague and complex than the *Songs of Innocence*.

4 An industry like this benefits everyone, from the poor, for whom it creates employment; to the rich, who are made richer by it.

This convention is the corollary of **66**. It cautions against using the semicolon to join elements of unequal rank. Accordingly, if there is an independent clause on one side of the semicolon, there must be a balancing independent clause on the other side.

In all of the examples above, a semicolon has been used to join units of *unequal* rank. In all four sentences, there is an independent clause on the *left-hand* side of the semicolon; however, there is no independent clause on the *right-hand* side of the semicolon in any of those sentences. What is on the right-hand side of the semicolon could be called a sentence fragment (see **29**).

Punctuation

In sentence **1**, there is the independent clause **she played the guitar expertly** on the left-hand side of the semicolon, but on the right-hand side of the semicolon, there is only the adverb clause **although she couldn't read a note of music**. That adverb clause belongs with, depends on, the first clause. Since it is an integral part of the first clause, it should be *joined* with that clause. The effect of the semicolon is to make the adverb clause part of *another* clause that begins after the semicolon. But on the right-hand side of the semicolon, there is no independent clause that the subordinate, dependent adverb clause can be a part of. One way to correct the sentence is to supply an independent clause, on the right-hand side of the semicolon, that the adverb clause can adhere to—e.g. **She played the guitar expertly; although she couldn't read a note of music, she simply had a knack for playing stringed instruments**. The other way to correct the sentence is to substitute a comma for the semicolon.

Sentences **2, 3,** and **4** could also be corrected by substituting a comma for the semicolon. But in **2**, it would probably be better to supply an independent clause on the right-hand side of the semicolon. So revised, the sentence would have an independent clause on *both* sides of the semicolon.

Here are the sample sentences revised:

1 She played the guitar expertly, although she couldn't read a note of music.

2 Americans spend far too many hours as spectators of sports instead of as participants in them; they spend far too many hours watching meaningless drivel on television instead of spending that time reading a book.

3 The two series of poems also differ in style, the *Songs of Experience* being more vague and complex than the *Songs of Innocence*.

4 An industry like this benefits everyone, from the poor, for whom it creates employment, to the rich, who are made richer by it.

68

Use a colon after a grammatically complete lead-in sentence that formally announces a subsequent enumeration, explanation, illustration, or extended quotation.

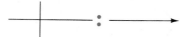

The following sentences either need a colon or use a colon improperly:

1 The courses I am taking this quarter are: English, sociology, economics, political science, and psychology.

2 His approach works like this ——— after displaying his product and extolling its virtues, he asks the homemaker if she has a small rug that she would like to have cleaned.

3 Examples of the diction used to evoke the horror of the scene include vivid images like: "coughing like hags," "thick green light," "guttering," "white eyes writhing in his face," "gargling from froth-corrupted lungs."

4 The reaction of the crowd signified only one thing , apathy.

A colon signals that what *follows* it is a specification of what was formally announced in the clause on the left-hand side of the colon. What distinguishes the colon from the dash as a symbolic device is that the colon throws the reader's attention *forward*, whereas the dash as a linking device throws the reader's attention *backward* (see **69**). Although a word, a phrase, or a clause or a series of words, phrases, or clauses can follow the colon, there must be an independent clause (a grammatically complete sentence) on the left-hand side of the colon.

Punctuation

In accord with this principle, sentence **1** should not have been punctuated the way it was; that punctuation makes no more sense than punctuating a sentence in this way:

My name is: John Adams.

In both cases, the words following the colon are needed to complete the sentence grammatically. So either the colon must be dropped altogether, or enough words must be added to make the clause on the left-hand side of the colon a grammatically complete sentence—in sentence **1**, *are these* or *are as follows*.

In sentence **3**, the quoted phrases following the colon are needed to complete the prepositional phrase that begins with **like**. Therefore, either drop the colon or add a completing word like **these** before the colon. Since the lead-in clause in sentence **2** throws the reader's attention forward, the dash after **this** should be replaced by a colon. Likewise, the comma in the fourth sentence should be replaced by a colon.

A colon is conventionally used after the lead-in sentence that introduces an extended quotation in a research paper. Here is an example of that use:

Toward the end of the preface, Dr. Johnson confessed that he abandoned his earlier expectation that his dictionary would be able to "fix the language":

Those who have been persuaded to think well of my design will require that it should fix our language and put a stop to those alterations which time and chance have hitherto been suffered to make in it without opposition. With this consequence I will confess that I flattered myself for a while, but now begin to fear that I have indulged expectation which neither reason nor experience can justify.

Here are the sample sentences properly punctuated with a colon:

1 The courses I am taking this quarter are as follows: English, sociology, economics, political science, and psychology.

2 His approach works like this: after displaying his product and extolling its virtues, he asks the homemaker if she has a small rug that she would like to have cleaned.

3 Examples of the diction used to evoke the horror of the scene include vivid images like these: "coughing like hags," "thick green light," "guttering," "white eyes writhing in his face," "gargling from froth-corrupted lungs."

4 The reaction of the crowd signified only one thing: apathy.

69

Use a dash when the word or word-group that follows it constitutes a summation, an amplification, or a reversal of what went before it.

Examples of sentences that need to be punctuated with a dash:

1 English, psychology, history, and philosophy, these were the courses I took last quarter.

2 If he was pressured, he would become sullen and tight-lipped, a reaction that did not endear him to the president or the Senate.

3 Time and time again, she would admit that her critics were right, that she should have realized her mistakes, that she should have read the danger signs more accurately and then gone ahead with her original plans.

Unlike the colon (see **68**), which directs the reader's attention forward, the dash usually directs the reader's attention back-

Punctuation

ward. What follows the dash, when it is used as a linking device, looks back to what preceded it for the particulars or details that spell out the meaning or invest the meaning with pungency or irony.

The colon and the dash are usually not interchangeable marks of punctuation. They signal a different relationship between the word-groups that precede them and those that follow them. After much practice in writing, one develops a sense for the subtle distinction in relationships that is signaled by the punctuation in the following two sentences:

> The reaction of the crowd signified only one thing: apathy.
>
> The people clearly indicated their indifference to the provocative speech—an apathy that later came back to haunt them.

In the first sentence, the lead-in clause before the colon clearly alerts the reader to expect a specification of what is hinted at in that clause. In the second sentence, there is no such alerting of the reader in the lead-in clause; but following the dash, there is an unexpected commentary on what was said in the lead-in clause, a summary commentary that forces the reader to look backward and that receives a special emphasis by being set off with a dash. The colon and the single dash are both linking devices, but they signal different kinds of thought relationships between parts of the sentence.

Writers should also be cautioned to avoid using the dash as a catchall mark of punctuation, one that is indiscriminately substituted for periods, commas, semicolons, etc.

Here now are the sample sentences with a dash inserted in the proper place:

1 English, psychology, history, and philosophy—these were the courses I took last quarter.

2 If he was pressured, he would become sullen and tight-lipped—a reaction that did not endear him to the president or the Senate.

3 Time and time again, she would admit that her critics were right, that she should have realized her mistakes, that she should have read the danger signs more accurately—and then gone ahead with her original plans.

70

Use a pair of dashes to enclose abrupt parenthetical elements that occur within a sentence.

Examples of parenthetical elements that should be enclosed with a pair of dashes:

1 In some instances, although no one will admit it, the police over-reacted to the provocation.

2 What surprised everyone when the measure came to a vote was the chairperson's reluctance, indeed, downright refusal, to allow any riders to be attached to the bill.

3 One of them (let me call him Jim Prude) is clean-shaven and dresses like an Ivy Leaguer of the early 1950s.

4 Their unhappiness is due to the ease with which envy is aroused and to the difficulty, or should I say impossibility, of fighting against it.

5 Yet despite the similarities in their travelogues (for indeed the same trip inspired both works), the two reports differ in some key aspects.

The three devices used to set off parenthetical elements in written prose are commas, parentheses, and dashes. The kind of parenthetical element that should be enclosed with a pair of dashes is the kind that interrupts the normal syntactical flow of the sentence. What characterizes all of the parenthetical elements in the examples above is that they abruptly arrest the

Punctuation

normal flow of the sentence to add some qualifying or rectifying comment. The rhetorical effect of the enclosing dashes is to alert the reader to the interruption and thereby to help the reader read the sentence.

A pair of parentheses is another typographical device used to mark off parenthetical elements in a sentence. Enclosure within parentheses is used mainly for those elements that merely add information or identification, as in sentences like these:

> All the companies that used the service were charged a small fee (usually $500) and were required to sign a contract (an "exclusive-use" agreement).

> The manager of each franchise is expected to report monthly to NARM (National Association of Retail Merchants) and to "rotate" (take turns doing various jobs) every two weeks.

The typographical device used to set off the mildest kind of interrupting element is a pair of commas. Whether to enclose a parenthetical element with commas or with parentheses or with dashes is often more a matter of stylistic choice than a matter of grammatical necessity. There are degrees of interruption and emphasis, and with practice, a writer develops an instinct for knowing when to mark off parenthetical elements with commas (lowest degree of interruption and emphasis), when to mark them off with parentheses (middle degree), and when to mark them off with dashes (highest degree). Consider the degrees of interruption and emphasis in the following sentences:

> That agency, as we have since learned, reported the incident directly to the Department of Justice.

> During the postwar years (at least from 1946 to 1952), no one in the agency dared challenge a directive from higher up.

> When the order was challenged, the attorney general—some claim it was his wife—put a call through to the president.

Here are the revisions of the sample sentences with the parenthetical elements enclosed with dashes:

1 In some instances—although no one will admit it—the police overreacted to the provocation.

2 What surprised everyone when the measure came to a vote was the chairperson's reluctance—indeed, downright refusal—to allow any riders to be attached to the bill.

3 One of them—let me call him Jim Prude—is clean-shaven and dresses like an Ivy Leaguer of the early 1950s.

4 Their unhappiness is due to the ease with which envy is aroused and to the difficulty—or should I say impossibility—of fighting against it.

5 Yet despite the similarities in their travelogues—for indeed the same trip inspired both works—the two reports differ in some key aspects.

71

A dash is made on the typewriter with two unspaced hyphens and with no space before the dash or after the dash. (In handwriting, the dash should be made slightly longer than a hyphen.)

Examples of incorrect ways of forming the dash on a typewriter:

```
She forgot-if she ever knew-the functions of
the various marks of punctuation.
```

Punctuation

```
She forgot - if she ever knew - the functions of
the various marks of punctuation.

She forgot -- if she ever knew -- the functions
of the various marks of punctuation.

She forgot - - if she ever knew - - the func-
tions of the various marks of punctuation.
```

Because a typewriter does not have a separate key for a dash, you have to make a dash with two hyphens. Do not hit the spacebar on the typewriter before the first hyphen, *between* the first and second hyphen, or *after* the second hyphen. In short, do not hit the spacebar at all in forming the dash on the typewriter. When you are handwriting a text, you have to distinguish a dash from a hyphen by making the dash slightly longer than the hyphen.

Here is an illustration of the proper way to form the dash on the typewriter:

```
She forgot--if she ever knew--the functions of
the various marks of punctuation.
```

Mechanics

The graphic devices dealt with in this section might be, and often are, classified as punctuation. But because such graphic devices as italics, capitalization, and numbers are not correlated—as punctuation marks are—with the intonational patterns of the spoken language, these devices are grouped in a separate section under the heading Mechanics. In the spoken language, a word printed with an initial capital letter is pronounced no differently from the same word printed with an initial lower-case letter. Nor is the italicized title of a book pronounced any differently from that same title printed without italics. (Italics used for emphasizing a word or phrase, however, do correspond to stress in the spoken language.) Even quotation marks, which one might regard as correlated with the spoken language, do not correspond to anything the voice does when it quotes direct speech.

But whether one classifies these graphic devices as punctuation or as mechanics is immaterial. What is important to remember is that these devices are part of the written language exclusively and that they facilitate the reading of that language.

Mechanics

Most readers would have at least momentary difficulty making sense of the following string of words:

> Jill cried buckets as many as you can fetch Jack thought I don't have to please you over there she continued nuts pails they're called yelled Jack

If the proper punctuation and mechanics were used with that string of words, readers would be spared the momentary difficulty:

> Jill cried, "Buckets! As many as you can fetch!" Jack thought, "I don't have to!" "Please, you over there!" she continued. "Nuts! *pails* they're called!" yelled Jack.

Deprived of the resources that the human voice possesses to clarify the meaning of words as spoken, writers should be eager to use all those typographical devices that make it easier for readers to grasp what the writers are trying to convey.

80

The period or the comma always goes inside the closing quotation mark.

Examples of sentences with misplaced quotation marks:

1 The author announces at the beginning of her article that she is going to cite only "facts".

2 "I know," she said, "that you are telling me a barefaced lie".

3 Mrs. Robinson's "bearded, sandaled, unwashed hippies", many of whom had traveled over a thousand miles to the festival, represented an aggregation of straight-*A* students.

80 Closing Quotation Mark, with Period and Comma

This is a clear case where usage, rather than logic, has established the prevailing convention. Many reputable British editors and publishers put the period or comma *outside* the closing quotation mark, especially when the quotation marks enclose something less than a complete sentence—e.g. a word or a phrase, such as in sentences **1** and **3** above. But the American convention is almost universally to put the period or comma *inside* the closing quotation mark.

The advantage of such consistency is that you never have to pause and ask yourself, "Is this a case where the period goes inside or outside the quotation mark?" Whether it is a single word or a phrase or a dependent clause or an independent clause, the period or comma always goes *inside* the closing quotation mark.

In handwriting or in typewriting, take care to put the period or comma *clearly* inside the quotation mark, not *under* it, as in sentence **2**. In the case of a quotation within a quotation, both the single-stroke quotation mark and the double-stroke quotation mark go *outside* the period or the commas, as in this example:

> "I read recently," he said, "that Patrick Henry never said, 'Give me liberty or give me death."

Here are the revisions of the sample sentences with the proper placement of the closing quotation mark in relation to the period or the comma:

1 The author announces at the beginning of her article that she is going to cite only "facts."

2 "I know," he said, "that you are telling me a barefaced lie."

3 Mrs. Robinson's "bearded, sandaled, unwashed hippies," many of whom had traveled over a thousand miles to the festival, represented an aggregation of straight-*A* students.

Mechanics

81

The colon or semicolon always goes outside the closing quotation mark.

’’: ’’;

Examples of a misplaced colon or semicolon in relation to the closing quotation mark:

1 She called this schedule of activities her "load:" work, study, exercise, recreation, and sleep.

2 He told his taunters, "I refuse to budge;" his knees, however, were shaking even as he said those words.

Whereas the period or the comma always goes *inside* the closing quotation mark, the colon or the semicolon always goes outside it. Whenever writers have occasion to use quotation marks with a colon or a semicolon, they have only to recall that the convention governing the relationship of the colon or the semicolon to the closing quotation mark is just the opposite of the convention for the period and the comma.

Here are the revisions of the sample sentences with the colon and the semicolon placed in the right position in relation to the closing quotation mark:

1 She called this schedule of activities her "load"’’: work, study, exercise, recreation, and sleep.

2 He told his taunters, "I refuse to budge"’’; his knees, however, were shaking even as he said those words.

82

The question mark sometimes goes inside, sometimes outside, the closing quotation mark.

?"   "?

Examples of the question mark placed wrongly in relation to the closing quotation mark:

1 Who was it that said, "I regret that I have but one life to lose for my country?"

2 He asked her bluntly, "Will you marry me"?

3 When will they stop asking, "Who then is responsible for the war"?

Although a period or a comma always goes inside the closing quotation mark and a colon or a semicolon always goes outside it, you have to consider each case individually before deciding whether to put the question mark inside or outside the closing quotation mark. Fortunately, the criteria for determining whether it goes inside or outside the quotation mark are fairly simple to apply:

(a)   When the whole sentence, but not the unit enclosed in quotation marks, is a question, the question mark goes *outside* the closing quotation mark. (See sentence **1**.)

(b)   When only the unit enclosed in quotation marks is a question, the question mark goes *inside* the closing quotation mark. (See sentence **2**.)

(c)   When the whole sentence and the unit enclosed in quotation marks are both questions, the question mark goes *inside* the closing quotation mark. (See sentence **3**.)

Whenever the question mark occurs at the end of a sentence, it serves as the terminal punctuation for the entire sen-

Mechanics

tence. In **(b)**, you do not add a period outside the closing quotation mark, and in **(c)**, you do not add another question mark outside the closing quotation mark.

Here are the sample sentences corrected in accord with the criteria set forth in **(a)**, **(b)**, and **(c)**:

1 Who was it that said, "I regret that I have but one life to lose for my country"?

2 He asked her bluntly, "Will you marry me?"

3 When will they stop asking, "Who then is responsible for the war?"

83

The titles of books, newspapers, magazines, professional journals, plays, long poems, movies, radio programs, television programs, long musical compositions, works of art, and the names of ships and airplanes should be *underlined*.

Examples of titles that should be underlined:

1 The critics have always rated Hemingway's "A Farewell to Arms" above his "For Whom the Bell Tolls."

2 To support her contention, she quoted a passage from an anonymous article in Newsweek.

3 My parents insisted on watching "All in the Family."

4 Charles Darwin took a historic trip on the Beagle.

Printers use *italics*—a special typeface that slants slightly to the right—to set off certain words in a sentence (or certain sentences in a paragraph) from the body of words or sentences, which are printed in roman type (upright letters). The word *italics* in this and the previous sentence is printed in italics. In handwriting or typewriting, one italicizes words by underlining them.

One of the uses of italic type is to set off the words that appear in certain kinds of names and titles. Most often, writers have occasion to use italics for the titles of book- or pamphlet-length published materials. Besides being a convention, the use of italics for titles can also protect meaning in some instances. If someone wrote "I don't really like Huckleberry Finn," a reader might be uncertain (unless the context gave a clue) whether the writer was revealing a dislike for Mark Twain's novel or for the character of that name in the novel. Simply by underlining (italicizing) the proper name, the writer could indicate unambiguously that she or he disliked the novel, not the character.

How does one decide whether a poem is long enough to have its title underlined? As with most relative matters, the extreme cases are easily determinable. Obviously, a sonnet would not qualify as a long poem, but Milton's *Paradise Lost* would. It is the middle-length poem that causes indecision. A reliable rule of thumb is this: if the poem was ever published as a separate book or if it could conceivably be published as a separate book, it can be considered long enough to have its title underlined. According to that guideline, T. S. Eliot's *The Wasteland* would be considered a long poem, but his "The Love Song of J. Alfred Prufrock" would be considered a short poem and therefore should be enclosed in quotation marks (see **84**). But if you cannot decide whether a poem is "long" or "short," either underline the title or enclose it in quotation marks and use that system consistently throughout the paper.

Here are the sample sentences, with the titles underlined (italicized):

Mechanics

1 The critics have always rated Hemingway's <u>A Farewell to Arms</u> above his <u>For Whom the Bell Tolls.</u>

(titles of novels)

2 To support her contention, she quoted a passage from an anonymous article in <u>Newsweek.</u>

(title of a magazine)

3 My parents insisted on watching <u>All in the Family.</u>

(title of a television show)

4 Charles Darwin took a historic trip on the <u>Beagle.</u>

(name of a ship)

84

The titles of articles, essays, short poems, songs, and chapters of books should be enclosed in quotation marks.

Examples of titles that need to be enclosed with quotation marks:

1 Thomas Gray's Elegy Written in a Country Churchyard is reputed to be the most anthologized poem in the English language.

2 Hollis Alpert's <u>Movies Are Better Than the Stage</u> first appeared in the <u>Saturday Review of Literature.</u>

3 'Raindrops Keep Falling on My Head' set exactly the right mood for the bicycle caper in <u>Butch Cassidy and the Sundance Kid.</u>

The general rule here is that the titles of published material that is *part* of a book or a periodical should be enclosed in quotation marks.

The title of a paper that you write should not be enclosed in quotation marks, nor should it be underlined. If your title contains elements that are normally underlined or enclosed in quotation marks, those elements, of course, should be underlined or enclosed in quotation marks.

The right and the wrong formats of a title for a paper submitted as a class assignment or for publication are illustrated here in typescript:

WRONG: "The Evolution of Courtly Love in Medieval Literature"

The Evolution of Courtly Love in Medieval Literature

RIGHT: The Evolution of Courtly Love in Medieval Literature

The Evolution of Courtly Love in Chaucer's Troilus and Criseyde

Courtly Love in Herrick's "Corinna's Going a-Maying" and Marvell's "To His Coy Mistress"

The Shift in Meaning of the Word Love in Renaissance Lyrics

"One Giant Step for Mankind"--Historic Words for a Historic Occasion

Here are the revised sentences with the titles enclosed in quotation marks:

1 Thomas Gray's "Elegy Written in a Country Churchyard" is reputed to be the most anthologized poem in the English language.
(*title of a short poem*)

2 Hollis Alpert's "Movies Are Better Than the Stage" first appeared in the Saturday Review of Literature.
(*title of an article in a periodical*)

Mechanics

3 ""Raindrops Keep Falling on My Head" set exactly the right mood for the bicycle caper in Butch Cassidy and the Sundance Kid. (*title of a song*)

85

Underline (italicize) words referred to as words.

Examples of words that should be underlined (italicized).

1 She questioned the appropriateness of honesty in this context.

2 The American Heritage Dictionary defines dudgeon as "a sullen, angry, or indignant humor."

3 Unquestionably, trudged is a more specific verb than walked

4 Look, for example, at his use of purely subjective words like marvelous, exquisite, and wondrous

One of the uses of the graphic device of underlining (italics) is to distinguish a word being used *as a word* from that same word used as a symbol for a thing or an idea. Looking at two similar sentences can help us to see what difference in meaning is created by underlining or not underlining some word in the sentences:

She questioned the appropriateness of honesty in this context.

She questioned the appropriateness of honesty in this context.

Both of these sentences have the same words in the same order. The only difference between them is that in the second sentence, one of the words is underlined (italicized). That underlining of the word **honesty** makes for a difference in the meaning of the two sentences. The first sentence signifies that what is being challenged is the appropriateness of the thing (the abstract quality) designated by the word **honesty**; the second sentence signifies that what is being questioned is the appropriateness of the word only. Underlining (italicizing) the word **honesty** helps the reader to read the sentence as the writer intended it to be read—namely, that it was the word, not the virtue, that was being questioned.

An alternative but less common device for marking words used as words is to enclose the words in quotation marks, as in this example:

> The heavy use of such sensory diction as "juicy," "empurpled," "smooth," "creaked," "murmuring" helps to evoke the scene and make it palpable to the reader.

Since both devices are authorized by convention, the writer should adopt one system and use it consistently. The use of italics is probably the safer of the two systems, however, because quotation marks are also used to enclose quoted words and phrases, as in the sentence

> We heard her say "yes."

(Here **yes** is not being referred to as a word but is a quotation of what she said.)

Here are the sample sentences revised to include the underlining (italicizing) of words being referred to as words:

1 She questioned the appropriateness of honesty in this context.
2 The American Heritage Dictionary defines dudgeon as "a sullen, angry, or indignant humor."
3 Unquestionably, trudged is a more specific verb than walked.
4 Look, for example, at his use of purely subjective words like marvelous, exquisite, and wondrous.

86

Underline (italicize) foreign words and phrases, unless they have become naturalized or Anglicized.

Examples of foreign words and phrases that should be underlined (italicized):

1 Why does the advertiser, whose mouthpiece is the copywriter, allow himself to be presented before the public as a poet *malgré lui*?

2 The advice to begin a short story as close to the climax as possible is a heritage of Horace's advice to begin a narrative *in medias res* rather than *ab ovo*.

3 There had been a remarkable revival in the late 1960s of the *Weltschmerz* that characterized the poetry of the Romantics.

So that the reader will not be even momentarily mystified by the sudden intrusion of strange-looking words into a stream of English words, printers use italics to underscore foreign words and phrases. The graphic device of italics does not ensure, of course, that the reader will be able to translate the foreign expression, but it does prevent confusion by alerting the reader to the presence of non-English words.

Some foreign words and phrases, like habeas corpus, divorcee, mania, siesta, subpoena, have been used so often in an English context that they have been accepted into the vocabulary as "naturalized" English words and therefore as not needing to be underlined (italicized). Dictionaries have a system for indicating which foreign words and phrases have become naturalized and which have *not* become naturalized. Since dictionaries sometimes differ in their judgments about the naturalized status of certain foreign expressions, the writer in such doubtful cases may put the foreign word or phrase in ordinary (roman) type—that is, without underlining or italicizing.

An exception to the rule is that proper nouns designating foreign persons, places, and institutions, even when they retain their native spelling and pronunciation, are *always* set forth without underlining (italics).

Here are the sample sentences with their foreign words and phrases properly underlined:

1 Why does the advertiser, whose mouthpiece is the copywriter, allow himself to be presented before the public as a poet <u>malgré lui?</u>

2 The advice to begin a short story as close to the climax as possible is a heritage of Horace's advice to begin a narrative <u>in medias res</u> rather than <u>ab ovo.</u>

3 There had been a remarkable revival in the late 1960s of the <u>Welt-schmerz</u> that characterized the poetry of the Romantics.

87

Compound words should be hyphenated.

Examples of compound words that need to be hyphenated:

1 Because I had the normal **six year old's** "sweet tooth," I was irresistibly lured by the candy store.

2 She was attracted to **antiEstablishment** movements because they lacked **policy making** administrators.

3 They scheduled the examinations in three **quarter hour** segments.

4 She preferred **eighteenth century** literature because of its urbanity.

5 A **five** or **six story** building should be all you need for that kind of plant operation.

6 Jim Paisley was the only **new car** dealer in town.

Mechanics

English reveals its Germanic origins in its tendency to form compounds—that is, to take two or more words and join them to create a single unit that designates a thing or a concept quite different from what the individual words designate. A familiar example is the word basketball. When the two distinct words *basket* and *ball* were first joined to designate an athletic game or the kind of ball used in that game, the words were linked by a hyphen: *basket-ball*. When repeated use had made this new compound familiar to readers, the hyphen was dropped, and the two words were printed as a single word, with no break between the two constituent parts.

Dozens of words in English have made this transition from a hyphenated compound to a single amalgamated word (e.g. *postoffice, skyscraper, briefcase, airport*). But hundreds of compounds are still printed with a hyphen, either because they have not been used enough to achieve status as unmarked hybrids or because the absence of a hyphen would lead to ambiguity. A reliable dictionary will indicate which compounds have made the passage and which have not.

With the exception of those words that have become recognized amalgams, a hyphen should be used to link

(a) two or more words functioning as a single grammatical unit.

his **never-say-die** attitude (adjective)

the junkyard had a huge **car-crusher** (noun)

the hoodlums **pistol-whipped** him (verb)

he conceded the point **willy-nilly** (adverb)

(b) two-word numbers (from 21 to 99) when they are written out.

twenty-one, thirty-six, forty-eight, ninety-nine

(c) combinations with prefixes **ex-** and **self-**.

ex-president, ex-wife, self-denial, self-contradictory

(d)   combinations with prefixes like **anti-, pro-, pre-, post-,** when the second element in the combinations begins with a capital letter or a number.

anti-Establishment, pro-American, pre-1929, post-1945

(e)   combinations with prefixes like **anti-, pro-, pre-, re-, semi-, sub-, over-,** when the second element begins with the letter that occurs at the end of the prefix.

anti-intellectual, pro-oxidant, pre-election, re-entry, semi-independent, sub-basement, over-refined

(f)   combinations where the unhyphenated compound might be mistaken for another word.

re-cover (the chair)

recover (the lost wallet)

re-sign (the contract)

resign (the office)

co-op

coop

With the exceptions noted in **(d)** and **(e)**, compounds formed with prefixes now tend to be written as a single word (for example, *antiknock*, *preconscious*, *subdivision*, *postgraduate*). From extensive reading, one develops a sense for those compounds that have been used often enough to become a single word in English.

Frequently in writing, only a hyphen will clarify ambiguous syntax. In sentence 3, for instance, a reader would have difficulty determining whether the examination was divided into three segments of fifteen minutes each (a meaning that would be clearly signaled by this placement of the hyphen: **three quarter-hour segments**) or whether it was divided into segments of forty-five minutes duration (a meaning that is clearly

Mechanics

signaled by this placement of hyphens: **three-quarter-hour segments**). There is a similar ambiguity in sentence **6, Jim Paisley was the only new car dealer in town.** A speaker would be able to clarify the ambiguous syntax of that sentence by the appropriate intonation of the voice. But in writing, only a hyphen will make clear whether the writer meant to say that Jim Paisley was the only new **car-dealer** in town or that he was the only **new-car** dealer in town.

Sentence **5** shows how to hyphenate when there is more than one term on the left side of the hyphenation (**five-, six-**). In this way, **story** need not be repeated (as in **A five-story or six-story building. . .**). In typing, one inserts a space after the hyphen if the hyphen is not immediately followed by the word it is meant to join (**five- or;** NOT: **five-or**).

Here are the revisions of the sample sentences with the hyphens inserted in all the compound words:

1 Because I had the normal six‗year‗old's "sweet tooth," I was irresistibly lured by the candy store.

2 She was attracted to anti‗Establishment movements because they lacked policy‗making administrators.

3 They scheduled the examinations in three quarter‗hour segments.

4 She preferred eighteenth‗century literature because of its urbanity.

5 A five‗ or six‗story building should be all you will need for that kind of plant operation.

6 Jim Paisley was the only new‗car dealer in town.

88

A word can be broken and hyphenated at the end of a line only at a syllable-break; a one-syllable word can never be broken and hyphenated.

Examples of words improperly syllabified:

1 bell-igerent
2 stopp-ing
3 rigo-rous
4 a-bout
5 comm-unity
6 wrench-ed

For the writer, two valuable bits of information are supplied by the initial entry of every word in the dictionary: (1) the spelling of the word, (2) the syllabification of the word. The word **belliger-ent**, for instance, is entered this way in the dictionary: **bel·lig-er·ent**. If that word occurred at the end of a line and you saw that you could not get the whole word in the remaining space, you could break the word and hyphenate it at any of the syllables marked with a raised period. But you could not break the word in any of the following places: **bell·igerent, belli·gerent, bellige·rent**.

Since the syllabification of English words is often unpredictable, it is safest to consult a dictionary when you are in doubt about where syllable-breaks occur. But after a while, you learn certain "tricks" about syllabification that save you a trip to the dictionary. A word can usually be broken

(a)   after a prefix (**con-, ad-, un-, im-**).
(b)   before a suffix (**-tion, -ment, -less, -ous, -ing**).

Mechanics

(c) between double consonants (**oc·cur·rence, cop·per, stop·ping, prig·gish**).

One-syllable words, however, can never be divided and hy-phenated, no matter how long they are. So if you come to the end of a line and find that you do not have enough space to squeeze in single-syllable words like **horde, grieve, stopped, quaint, strength, wrenched,** leave the space blank and write the whole word on the next line. You have no choice.

Even in the interest of preserving a right-hand margin, you should not divide a word so that only one or two letters of it stand at the end of the line or at the beginning of the next line. Faced with divisions like **a·bout, o·cean, un·healthy, grass·y, dioram·a, flor·id, smok·er, live·ly,** you should put the whole word on that line or on the next line. Remember that the hyphen itself takes up one space.

Here are the sample words hyphenated in the right place or not syllabified at all:

1 bel·lig·er·ent
2 stop·ping
3 rigor·ous
4 about
5 com·mu·ni·ty
6 wrenched

89

Observe the conventions governing the use of numbers in written copy.

Examples of violations of the conventions:

1 **522** men reported to the recruiting center.

2 During the first half of the **20th** century, **28 4**-year colleges and **14 2**-year colleges adopted collective-bargaining agencies.

3 The cocktail party started at **four P.M. in the afternoon.**

4 An account of the Wall Street crash of October **twenty-ninth, nineteen hundred and twenty-nine** begins on page **fifty-five**.

5 About **six and a half** % of the stores were selling a gross of **three-by-five** index cards for more than **thirty-six dollars and thirty-eight cents**.

The most common conventions governing the use of numbers in written copy are as follows:

(a) Do not begin a sentence with an arabic numeral; spell out the number or recast the sentence:

Five hundred twenty-two men reported to the recruiting center.

OR: A total of **522** men reported to the recruiting center.

(b) Spell out any number of less than three digits (or any number under 101) when the number is used as an adjective modifying a noun:

During the first half of the **twentieth** century, **twenty-eight four**-year colleges and **fourteen two**-year colleges adopted collective-bargaining agencies.

(c) Always use arabic numerals with A.M. and P.M. and do not add the redundant **o'clock** and **morning** or **afternoon**:

The cocktail party started at **4:00** P.M.

OR: The cocktail party started at **four o'clock in the afternoon.**

(d) Use arabic numerals for dates and page numbers:

An account of the Wall Street crash of October **29, 1919** begins on page **55**.

(e) Use arabic numerals for addresses (618 N. 29th St.), dollars and cents ($4.68, $0.15 or 15 cents), decimals (3.14,

Mechanics

0.475), degrees (52°F.), measurements (especially when abbreviations are used: 3″ × 5″, 3.75 mi., 2 ft. 9 in., 6′2″ tall, but
six feet tall), percentages (6% or 6 percent, but always use **percent** with fractional percentages—6½ percent or 6.5 percent):

> About **6½ percent** of the stores were selling a gross of **3** ″ × **5** ″ in-
> dex cards for more than **$36.38.**

90

Observe the conventions governing the capitalization of certain words.

Examples of words that need to be capitalized:

1 president Gerald R. Ford informed the members of congress that he
was appointing ms. Shirley Temple Black as the united states ambassador to ghana.

2 The title of the article in the *New Yorker* was "The time of illusion."

3 Dr. Thomas J. Cade, a professor in the division of biological sciences at Cornell university, has been supervising the breeding of
peregrines captured in the arctic, the west, and the pacific northwest.

4 The prime vacation time for most Americans is the period between
the fourth of July and labor day.

5 The korean troops resisted the incursion of the communist forces.

In general, the convention governing capitalization is that the
first letter of the proper name (that is, the particular or exclusive
name) of persons, places, things, institutions, agencies, etc.
should be capitalized. While the tendency today is to use lower-
case letters for many words that formerly were written or
printed with capital letters (for instance, *biblical reference* in-

stead of *Biblical reference*), the use of capital letters still prevails in the following cases:

(a) The first letter of the first word of a sentence.

They were uncertain about which words should be capitalized.

(b) The first letter of the first word of every line of English verse.

Little fly,
Thy summer's play
My thoughtless hand
Has brushed away.

(c) All nouns, pronouns, verbs, adjectives, adverbs, and first and last words of titles of publications and other artistic works.

Remembrance of Things Past (see **83**)
"**T**he **P**lace of the **E**nthymeme in **R**hetorical **T**heory" (see **84**)
"**A T**ent **T**hat **F**amilies **C**an Live **I**n"
The Return of the Pink Panther

(d) The first name, middle name or initial, and last name of a person, real or fictional.

T. S. Eliot
David **C**opperfield

Sylvia **M**arie **M**ikkelsen
Achilles

(e) The names and abbreviations of villages, towns, cities, counties, states, nations, and regions.

Chillicothe, **O**hio
U.S.A.
Indo-**C**hina

Franklin **C**ounty
Soviet **U**nion
Arctic **C**ircle

Mechanics

the **W**estern **W**orld | **S**outh **A**merica
the **M**idwestern states | the **S**outh (but: we drove south)

(f) The names of rivers, lakes, falls, oceans, mountains, deserts, parks.

the **M**ississippi **R**iver | **A**tlantic
the **G**rand **T**etons | **Y**ellowstone **N**ational **P**ark
Lake **E**rie | **V**ictoria **F**alls

(g) The names and abbreviations of businesses, industries, institutions, agencies, schools, political parties, religious denominations, and philosophical, literary, and artistic movements.

University of **N**ebraska | **D**emocrats
the **R**epublican convention | **C.I.A.**
Dow **C**hemical **C**orporation | **J**ohn **W**iley & **S**ons, **P**ublishers
Communist(s) (but: a communist ideology) | **S**mithsonian **I**nstitution
Victorian literature | **J**apan **A**ir **L**ines
Thomistic philosophy | the **P**entagon
| **P**ure **L**and **B**uddhism

(h) The titles of historical events, epochs, and periods.

Renaissance | **T**hirty **Y**ears' **W**ar
World **W**ar II | **I**ce **A**ge
the **M**iddle **A**ges | the **B**attle of **G**ettysburg
Reformation | the **D**epression

(i) Honorary and official titles when they precede the name of the person.

Rabbi **B**alfour **B**rickner | **B**ishop **T**suji
the **D**uke of **C**ornwall | **G**eneral **P**atton

156

Pope John Paul II   the Chief Justice
His (Her) Excellency   Queen Elizabeth

(j)   The names of weekdays, months, holidays, holy days, and other special days or periods.

Christmas Eve   Memorial Day
Passover   the Fourth of July
Lent   National Book Week
Mardi **Gras**   the first Sunday in June

(k)   The names and abbreviations of the books and divisions of the Bible and other sacred books (no italics for these titles).

Genesis   Pentateuch
Matt. (Gospel of Matthew)   Acts of the Apostles
Epistle to the Romans   Koran
King James Version   Scriptures
Talmud   Bhagavad Gita
Book of Job   Lotus Sutra
Pss. (Psalms)   Science and Health

Exceptions: Do not capitalize words like the underlined in the following examples:

the African coast (but: the   the river Elbe (but: the Elbe
West Coast)   River)
northern Wisconsin   the federal government
the senator from Wyoming   the presidential itinerary
the municipal library   the county courthouse

Here are the revisions of the sample sentences, with all the proper names capitalized:

1 President Gerald R. Ford informed the members of Congress that

Never-Say Neverisms

he was appointing Ms. Shirley Temple Black as the United States ambassador to Ghana.

2 The title of the article in the *New Yorker* was "The Time of Illusion."

3 Dr. Thomas J. Cade, a professor in the Division of Biological Sciences at Cornell University, has been supervising the breeding of peregrines captured in the Arctic, the West, and the Pacific Northwest.

4 The prime vacation time for most Americans is the period between the Fourth of July and Labor Day.

5 The Korean troops resisted the incursion of the Communist forces.

Never-Say Neverisms

William Safire

(If you have absorbed the lessons of this handbook, you will be able to detect what is wrong in each of the following proscriptions, which William Safire calls "never-say neverisms."*)

1. Remember to never split an infinitive.

2. The passive voice should never be used.

3. Avoid run-on sentences they are hard to read.

4. Don't use no double negatives.

5. Use the semicolon properly, always use it where it is appropriate; and never where it isn't.

6. Reserve the apostrophe for it's proper use and omit it when its not needed.

7. Do not put statements in the negative form.

8. Verbs has to agree with their subjects.

9. No sentence fragments.

*From William Safire, "The Fumblerules of Grammar," *The New York Times Magazine*, November 4, 1979, p.16, and "Fumblerule Follow-Up," November 25, 1979, p. 14. © 1979 by The New York Times Company. Reprinted by permission.

10. Proofread carefully to see if you any words out.

11. Avoid commas, that are not necessary.

12. If you reread your work, you will find on rereading that a great deal of repetition can be avoided by rereading and editing.

13. A writer must not shift your point of view.

14. Eschew dialect, irregardless.

15. And don't start a sentence with a conjunction.

16. Don't overuse exclamation marks!!!

17. Place pronouns as close as possible, especially in long sentences, as of ten or more words, to their antecedents.

18. Hyphenate between syllables and avoid un-necessary hyphens.

19. Write all adverbial forms correct.

20. Don't use contractions in formal writing.

21. Writing carefully, dangling participles must be avoided.

22. It is incumbent on us to avoid archaisms.

23. If any word is improper at the end of a sentence, a linking verb is.

24. Steer clear of incorrect forms of verbs that have snuck in the language.

25. Take the bull by the hand and avoid mixed metaphors.

26. Avoid trendy locutions that sound flaky.

27. Never, ever use repetitive redundancies.

28. Everyone should be careful to use a singular pronoun with singular nouns in their writing.

29. If I've told you once, I've told you a thousand times, resist hyperbole.

30. Also, avoid awkward or affected alliteration.

31. Don't string too many prepositional phrases together unless you are walking through the valley of the shadow of death.

32. Never use a long word when a diminutive one will do.

Never-Say Neverisms

33. If a dependent clause precedes an independent clause put a comma after the dependent clause.

34. One will not have needed the future perfect in one's entire life.

35. Unqualified superlatives are the worst of all.

36. If this were subjunctive, I'm in the wrong mood.

37. Always pick on the correct idiom.

38. "Avoid overuse of 'quotation "marks." ' "

39. The adverb always follows the verb.

40. Last but not least, avoid clichés like the plague; seek viable alternatives.

41. Surly grammarians insist that all words ending in "ly" are adverbs.

42. De-accession euphemisms.

43. In statements involving two word phrases, make an all out effort to use hyphens.

44. It is not resultful to transform one part of speech into another by prefixing, suffixing, or other alterings.

45. Avoid colloquial stuff.

Format of the Research Paper

General Instructions

A research paper reports the results of some investigation, experiment, interview, or reading that you have done. Some of the ordinary papers you write are also based on personal investigations, interviews, and reading, and when your paper is based on data derived from research, you should acknowledge the source of the data. For instance, you can reveal the source of information or quotations by saying, right in the text of your paper, "Mr. Stanley Smith, the director of the Upward Bound project, with whom I talked last week, confirmed the rumor that. . ." or "James Reston said in his column in last Sunday's *New York Times* that. . . ." Authors of research papers also use identifying lead-ins like those, but in addition, they supply—usually in footnotes—any further bibliographical information (such as the exact date of the newspaper they are quoting from and the number of the page from which the quotation was taken) that readers would need if they wanted to check the sources. By revealing this specific information about the source, authors enable readers to check whether they have been accurate or fair in their reporting, and they also enhance their credibility with readers.

Format of the Research Paper

In the pages that follow, we will present some advice about gathering and reporting material from outside sources, some models of footnote bibliography forms, and a sample reseach paper. The instructor or the publication that you write for may prescribe a format that differs from the advice given here, but if no specific instructions are given, you can follow these suggestions and models with the assurance that they conform to the prevailing conventions for research papers written in most fields. The format for documenting references, citations, and quotations may differ slightly from discipline to discipline, but whether you are writing a research paper in the humanities or in the physical sciences or in the social sciences, the same kind of basic information about the sources is supplied in the documentation.

(A) GATHERING NOTES

If you do enough research, you will eventually discover a system of gathering notes that works best for you. Some people, for instance, just scribble their notes on full sheets of paper or in spiral notebooks. Others record their notes and quotations on 3 × 5 or 4 × 6 cards—*one* note or quotation to a card. The advantage of recording notes on separate cards is that later you can select and arrange the cards to suit the order in which you are going to use them in your paper. It is considerably more difficult to select and arrange notes if they are written out, one after the other, on full sheets of paper. You could, of course, cut out notes from the full sheets, but that activity involves you in an extra step.

(B) SELF-CONTAINED NOTECARDS

Each notecard should be self-contained—that is, it should con-

What Needs to Be Footnoted?

tain all the information you would need to document that material properly if you used it in your paper. A notecard is self-contained if you never have to go back to the original source to recover any bit of information about the note. So each notecard should carry at least this much information:

1 The card should indicate whether the note is paraphrased or quoted verbatim. Don't trust your memory to be able to distinguish later whether a note is paraphrased or quoted.

2 If quoted material covers more than one page in the source from which it was copied, you should devise some system of indicating just where the quoted material went over to the next page. If later you use only part of that quotation, you have to know whether to cite one page (p. 189) or two pages (pp. 189–90) in the footnote. Some notation like **(→p. 190)** inserted in the notecard after the last word on the page (in this case, after the last word on p. 189) in the original source will help you determine later whether you need to cite one page or two pages.

3 The notecard should contain all the bibliographical information needed to document the note in a footnote of your paper: name of the author, title of the book or article, publication information, and page numbers (see MODEL FOOTNOTES, pp. 172–179). If you are taking several notes from the same source, you can devise some shorthand system so that you do not have to write out all the bibliographical information on every notecard.

(C) WHAT NEEDS TO BE FOOTNOTED?

You will have to develop a sense for what needs to be documented with a footnote. Here are some guidelines to help you:

1 Ordinarily, every direct quotation should carry a footnote. However, if you were doing a research paper on, say, a novel, you could be spared having to document every quotation from the novel by using a footnote like this the *first time* you quoted from the novel:

Format of the Research Paper

> [8]John Steinbeck, The Grapes of Wrath (New York: Viking Press, 1939), p. 134. Hereafter all quotations from this first edition of the novel will be documented with a page number in parentheses immediately after the quotation.

2 Paraphrased material may or may not need a footnote. If the fact or information that you report in your own words is *generally known* by people knowledgeable on the subject, you probably need not document that paraphrased material. For instance, if you were writing a research paper on the assassination of Abraham Lincoln, you probably would not have to document your statement that John Wilkes Booth shot Lincoln in Ford's Theater in Washington in April of 1865, because that historical fact is common knowledge. But if one of the arguments in your paper concerned the *exact time of the day* when he was shot, you would have to document your statement that Lincoln was shot at 8:40 P.M. on the evening of April 14, 1865. When, however, you cannot resolve your doubt about whether paraphrased material needs to be documented with a footnote that reveals the source of the information, document it.

3 When you are summarizing, in your own words, a great deal of information that you have gathered from your reading, you can be spared having to document several sentences in that summary by putting a footnote number after the *first sentence* of the summary and using a footnote like this:

> [10]For the biographical information presented in this and the subsequent paragraph, I am indebted to Minnie M. Brashear, Mark Twain: Son of Missouri (Chapel Hill: University of

North Carolina Press, 1934), pp. 34-65, and
Gamaliel Bradford, "Mark Twain," <u>Atlantic
Monthly</u>, 125 (April 1920), 462-73.

(D) KEEP QUOTATIONS TO A MINIMUM

A research paper should not be just a pastiche of long quotations stitched together by an occasional comment or by a transitional sentence by the author of the paper. You should use your own words as much as possible, and when you do quote, you should keep the quotation brief. Often a quoted phrase or sentence will make a point more emphatically than a long quotation. You must learn to look for the phrase or sentence that represents the kernel of the quotation and to use that extract rather than the full quotation. Otherwise, the point you want to make with the quotation may be lost in all the verbiage. You will be more likely to keep your quotations short if you try to work most of them into the framework of your own sentence, like this:

Frank Ellis calls such an interpretation "the
biographical fallacy, the assumption that an
exact, one-to-one correspondence exists between the person who is imagined to be speaking the lines of the poem (the Spokesman) and
the historical personage who is known to have
written the poem."[12]

Format of the Research Paper

Sometimes, however, when you find it difficult to present the essential point in a short extract, you will have to quote something at greater length. Long quotations (two sentences or more) should be *inset* three or four spaces from the left-hand margin and *single-spaced*, with *no quotation marks enclosing the quotation,* like this:

> Frank Ellis offers this cogent argument to refute the charge that the Epitaph is not integrated with the rest of the poem:
>
>> The evidence for this is said to lie in the fact that there are disparities between the two accounts that are given of the Stonecutter, one by the aged Swain and the other in Epitaph. But it has never been pointed out that these disparities are deliberate and dramatic. The illiterate old rustic is unsympathetic. His disapproval has been softened no doubt by death, but it is still apparent that to him the Stonecutter seemed lazy, queer, unsociable, and probably crazy. But the Epitaph enables the reader to see around this characterization. For the Spokesman, who composed the Epitaph, is an outlander, a fellow poeta ignotus, and therefore unsympathetic.[15]

(E) USE A LEAD-IN FOR ALL QUOTATIONS

Every direct quotation should be accompanied by a lead-in phrase or clause, which at least identifies by name the person who is about to speak. But it further aids coherence if the lead-in also points up the pertinence of the subsequent quotation to what you have been talking about or to what you are going to talk about. Here are some typical identifying and orienting lead-ins:

> Edmund Wilson countered this charge by saying that "there is never any reason for supposing that anybody but the governess sees the ghosts."
>
> "It apparently did not occur to any of Wilson's critics," says Oscar Cargill in defense of Wilson's interpretation, "that James might have an adequate motive for disguising his purpose in the tale."
>
> Robert Heilman has this to say about Wilson's interpretation of Henry James's haunting story:

(Following this last lead-in would be either a single sentence enclosed in quotation marks or a series of sentences inset and single-spaced, like the extended quotation in [D] above.)

(F) THE FORMAT OF FOOTNOTES

The first line of every footnote is indented from the left-hand margin (usually the same number of spaces as paragraph indentations in the body of the paper), but any subsequent lines of the same footnote are brought out to the left-hand margin. If footnotes are put at the bottom of the page, they are single-spaced *within* the footnote and double-spaced *between* footnotes. If footnotes are put on separate pages, they are double-spaced both *within* the footnote and *between* footnotes. See MODEL FOOTNOTES (pp. 172–179) and the sample research paper (pp. 187–200 and 211–214) for further information about the format of footnotes.

(G) PRIMARY AND SECONDARY FOOTNOTES

A *primary* footnote form (that is, those giving full bibliographical information) must be used the *first time* a source is cited. Thereafter, that same source can be documented with a *secondary* footnote form (that is, a shortened form). See MODEL FOOTNOTES (pp. 172–179) and the sample research papers on (pp.187–200) for the format of primary and secondary footnotes.

(H) THE FORMAT OF BIBLIOGRAPHICAL ENTRIES

Bibliographical entries are arranged alphabetically on separate pages at the end of the research paper. The list of entries is alphabetized according to the last name of the author (or, in the case of unsigned articles, according to the first significant word in the title). For that reason, the names of the authors are inverted in the bibliography—e.g. **Heilman, Robert.** The first line of each bibliographical entry begins at the left-hand margin, and any subsequent lines in that entry are indented (just the opposite of the format of footnotes). Bibliographical entries are single-spaced *within* the entry and double-spaced *between* entries. (If, however, the paper is being submitted for publication, the bibliographical entries are double-spaced both within the entry and between entries.) See MODELS FOR BIBLIOGRAPHY (pp.

180–186 and 207–210) for other differences between the format of footnotes and the format of bibliographical entries.

(l) ELLIPSIS PERIODS

Ellipsis periods (three spaced periods) are used to indicate that words or whole sentences have been omitted from a direct quotation:

```
The president said last week that "the Ameri-
can people . . . would not tolerate such vio-
lence."
```

(Note that there is a space between periods; wrong form: ...)

```
Philip Gove said in a letter to the New York
Times:

    The paragraph is, of course, a monstrosity,
    totally removed from possible occurrence in
    connection with any genuine attempt to use
    words in normally expected context. . . . A
    similar artificial monstrosity could be con-
    trived by jumbling together inappropriate
    words from formal literary language or from
    the Second Edition.
```

(The fourth period in this instance is the period used to mark the end of the sentence. Because of this period and the capital letter with which the next group of words begins, we know that at

Format of the Research Paper

least the end of the first sentence has been omitted and that
possibly several sentences or paragraphs have been removed
before the next sentence.)

Usually there is no need to put ellipsis periods at the beginning
or end of a quotation, because the reader knows that the quotation has been extracted from a larger context. Reserve ellipsis
periods for indicating omissions *within* quotations.

(J) SQUARE BRACKETS

Square brackets are used to enclose anything that the author of
the research paper inserts into a direct quotation:

```
About this tendency to indulge in scatological
language, H. A. Taine wrote, "He [Swift] drags
poetry not only through the mud, but into the
filth; he rolls in it like a raging madman, he
enthrones himself in it, and bespatters all
passers-by."


The Senator was emphatic in stating his reac-
tion to the measure: "This action by HEW
[Health, Education, and Welfare] will defi-
nitely not reverse the downward spiral [of
prices and wages] that has plagued us for the
last eight months."
```

We find this entry in the Japanese admiral's diary: "Promptly at 8:32 on Sunday morning of December 6 [sic], 1941, I dispatched the first wave of bombers for the raid on Perl Harber. [sic]."

(**Sic** *is a Latin adverb meaning "thus," "in this manner," and is used to let the reader know that the error in logic or fact or grammar or spelling in the quotation has been copied exactly as it was in the original source. It is italicized because it is a foreign word.*)

If your typewriter does not have keys that make square brackets, you will have to draw the brackets with a pen after you remove the paper from the typewriter, and so you should leave spaces for the brackets.

Format of the Research Paper: Model Footnotes

The models presented here for footnotes and for bibliography follow the forms prescribed in *The MLA Style Sheet,* 2nd ed. (New York: Modern Language Association, 1970), and in the much fuller *MLA Handbook* (New York: Modern Language Association, 1977). The MLA system of documentation is the most widely used system in America for scholarly manuscripts in the humanities.

The models presented throughout section (K) are single-spaced within the footnote and double-spaced between footnotes, as they would be if they appeared at the bottom of the page in a research paper or a dissertation. For the double-spacing of footnotes, see the MODEL FOR FOOTNOTES ENTERED ON SEPARATE PAGES (p. 200).

For the corresponding bibliography form for each of the model footnotes presented in section (K), see section (M) (pp. 181–186).

(K) PRIMARY FOOTNOTES

(the first reference to a source)

(1) A single book by a single author:

> [14]Hozen Seki, <u>The</u> <u>Great</u> <u>Natural</u> <u>Way</u> (New York: American Buddhist Academy, 1976), p. 88.

[8]John W. Landon, <u>Jesse Crawford: Poet of the Organ, Wizard of the Mighty Wurlitzer</u> (Vestal, NY: The Vestal Press, 1974), pp. 75-76.

(Notice that the first line of the footnote is indented and that subsequent lines of the footnote start at the left-hand margin. The **p.** *is the abbreviation of* **page;** **pp.** *is the abbreviation of* **pages***.)*

(2) A single book by more than one author:

[12]Paul A. Baran and Paul M. Sweezy, <u>Monopoly Capital</u> (New York: Monthly Review Press, 1966), p. 392.

(3) A book of more than one volume:

[13]William Lee Hays and Robert L. Winkler, <u>Statistics: Probability, Inference, and Decision</u> (New York: Holt, Rinehart & Winston, 1970), II, 137.

(Whenever a volume number is cited [here the Roman numeral **II**]*, the abbreviation* **p.** *or* **pp.** *is not used in front of the page number.)*

(4) A book edited by one or more editors:

[3]<u>Essays in American Economic History</u>, ed. Alfred W. Coats and Ross M. Robertson (London: Edward Arnold, 1969), pp. 268-9.

Format of the Research Paper

> [9]The Letters of Jonathan Swift to Charles
> Ford, ed. David Nichol Smith (Oxford: Clarendon
> Press, 1935), p. 187.

*(Here the abbreviation **ed.** stands for **edited by**.)*

(5) An essay or a chapter by an author in an edited
collection:

> [2]Martin J. Svaglic, "Classical Rhetoric and
> Victorian Prose," The Art of Victorian Prose,
> ed. George Levine and William Madden (New
> York: Oxford Univ. Press, 1968), pp. 268-70.

(6) A new edition of a book:

> [5]Oswald Doughty, A Victorian Romantic,
> Dante Gabriel Rossetti, 2nd ed. (London: Ox-
> ford Univ. Press, 1960), p. 35.

*(Here the abbreviation **ed.** stands for **edition**.)*

(7) A book that is part of a series:

> [26]William Heytesbury, Medieval Logic and
> the Rise of Mathematical Physics. University
> of Wisconsin Publications in Medieval Science,
> No. 3 (Madison: Univ. of Wisconsin Press, 1956),
> p. 97.

*(Here the abbreviation **No.** stands for **Number**.)*

(8) A book in a paperback series:

> [11]Edmund Wilson, <u>To the Finland Station</u>.
> Anchor Books (Garden City, NY: Doubleday,
> 1955), p. 130.

(9) A translation:

> [6]Fyodor Dostoevsky, <u>Crime and Punishment</u>,
> trans. Constance Garnett (New York: Heritage
> Press, 1938), p. 351.
>
> [7]Jacques Ellul, <u>A Critique of the New Com-
> monplaces</u>, trans. Helen Weaver (New York:
> Knopf, 1968), pp. 139-40.

*(The abbreviation **trans.** stands for **translated by**.)*

**(10) A signed and an unsigned article from an encyclo-
pedia:**

> [4]J. A. Ewing, "Steam-Engine and Other Heat-
> Engines," <u>Encyclopaedia Britannica</u>, 9th ed.,
> XXII, 475-7.
>
> [10]"Dwarfed Trees," <u>Encyclopedia Americana</u>,
> 1948, IX, 445.

*(Since encyclopedias periodically undergo revision and updat-
ing, the particular edition consulted should be indicated by a date
or a number. In the bibliography, unsigned articles are filed alphabetically according to the first significant word in the title—
here **Dwarfed**.)*

Format of the Research Paper

(11) An article from a journal:

[12]Nelson Adkins, "Emerson and the Bardic Tradition," PMLA, 72 (1948), 665.

[8]Theodore Otto Windt, Jr., "The Diatribe: Last Resort for Protest," QJS, 58 (1972), 9-10.

(Well-known scholarly journals are commonly referred to by their abbreviated titles. Here **PMLA** *stands for* **Publications of the Modern Language Association**; **QJS** *stands for* **Quarterly Journal of Speech**. *Volume numbers of journals are now designated by an Arabic number [here* **72** *and* **58**] *rather than, as formerly, by a Roman numeral. Because the volume number has been cited, the abbreviations* **p.** *and* **pp.** *are not used in front of the page numbers.)*

(12) An article in a popular magazine:

[4]Robert J. Levin, "Sex, Morality, and Society," Saturday Review, 9 July 1966, p. 29.

[7]Charles E. Silberman, "Technology Is Knocking on the Schoolhouse Door," Fortune, Aug. 1966, pp. 121-2.

(Note that **Saturday Review** *is a weekly magazine;* **Fortune** *is a monthly. Because no volume number is cited,* **p.** *and* **pp.** *are used in front of the page numbers.)*

176

(13) A signed and an unsigned article in a newspaper:

> [15]Art Gilman, "Altering U.S. Flag for Po-
> litical Causes Stirs a Legal Debate," <u>Wall
> Street Journal</u>, 12 June 1970, p. 1.
>
> [26]"Twin Games Bid: Wrestling, Judo," <u>New
> York Times</u>, 9 April 1972, Section 5, p. 15,
> cols. 4-6.

(For editions of a newspaper with multiple sections, each with its own pagination, it is necessary to cite the section in addition to the page number. It is helpful also to give column numbers. Sometimes, if an article appeared in one edition of a newspaper but not in other editions, it is necessary to specify the particular edition of the newspaper—e.g. **New York Times, Late City Ed., 4 Feb. 1972, p. 12, col.1***.)*

(14) A signed book review:

> [19]John F. Dalbor, rev. of <u>Meaning and Mind:
> A Study in the Psychology of Language</u>, by Rob-
> ert F. Terwilliger, <u>Philosophy & Rhetoric</u>, 5
> (1972), 60-61.
>
> [3]Brendan Gill, rev. of <u>Ibsen</u>, by Michael
> Meyer, New Yorker, 8 April 1972, p. 128.

(The first review appeared in a scholarly journal; the second review appeared in a weekly magazine. The abbreviation **rev.** *stands for* **review***.)*

Format of the Research Paper

(L) SECONDARY FOOTNOTES

(shortened forms after a source has once been given in full)

<blockquote>

[15]Seki, p. 80.

</blockquote>

(This is the shortened form of the first footnote given in (1) under Primary Footnotes.*)*

<blockquote>

[16]Hays and Winkler, II, 140.

</blockquote>

(This is the shortened form of the footnote given in (3) under Primary Footnotes.*)*

<blockquote>

[17]Ibid., I, 87.

</blockquote>

*(**Ibid.** is the abbreviation of the Latin adverb **ibidem**, meaning "in the same place." Ibid. may be used if the source in that footnote is the same as the one cited in the immediately preceding footnote. However, if a reader would have to turn back one or more pages to find the last source cited, it would be better to use the last-name shortened form: **Hays and Winkler, I, 87.** There must be added to Ibid. only what changes from the previous source. Thus in footnote **17** above, **1** and **87** were added to Ibid., because both the volume number and the page number changed from the previous footnote. If only the page number changed, footnote **17** would read thus: **Ibid., p. 145.** If nothing changed, footnote **17** would read thus: **Ibid.**)*

<blockquote>

[18]Wilson, <u>Finland Station</u>, pp. 220-2.

</blockquote>

Secondary Footnotes

*(When more than one book or article by the same author has been cited in a paper, you must use an abbreviated title in addition to the surname of the author in order to identify the source. In footnote **18** above, **Finland Station** is an abbreviated form of the full title, **To the Finland Station**.)*

[19]"Rendezvous with Ecology," p. 97.

(In the case of an anonymous article or book, the title or a shortened form of it must be used in subsequent references to that source.)

Format of the Research Paper

Format of the Research Paper: Models for Bibliography

The form of a bibliography entry differs in some ways from that of a footnote reference. The following shows how the two forms handle a citation for the same book:

BIBLIOGRAPHY FORM

```
Ryan, Edwin.  A College Handbook to Newman.
    Washington, DC: Catholic Education Press,
    1930.
```

FOOTNOTE FORM

```
    8Edwin Ryan, A College Handbook to
Newman (Washington, DC: Catholic Education
Press, 1930), p. 109.
```

The following lists, in parallel columns, point out the difference between the two forms:

BIBLIOGRAPHY	FOOTNOTE
(a) The first line begins at the left-hand margin, with all subsequent lines indented.	**(a)** The first line is indented, with all subsequent lines brought out to the left-hand margin.

BIBLIOGRAPHY	FOOTNOTE
(b) The name of the author is inverted (last name first) for purposes of alphabetizing the list of entries.	**(b)** The name of the author is set down in the normal order.
(c) The three main divisions (author, title, and publishing data) are separated by periods.	**(c)** The three main divisions (author, title, and publishing data) are separated by commas.
(d) Place of publication, name of the publisher, and publication date follow the title, without parentheses.	**(d)** Place of publication, name of the publisher, and publication date are enclosed in parentheses.
(e) The subtitle, if any, should be included in the citation. See (2) below.	**(e)** The subtitle, if any, may be omitted in the citation.
(f) There is no page reference unless the entry is for an article or part of a collection, in which case the full span of pages (first page and last page) is cited.	**(f)** Only a specific page reference is cited.

(M) CORRESPONDING BIBLIOGRAPHY FORMS FOR THE FOURTEEN MODEL FOOTNOTES

If the research paper is submitted as an assignment in a course, the bibliography entries may be single-spaced within

Format of the Research Paper

the entry and double-spaced between entries, as in the MODEL FOR A BIBLIOGRAPHY PAGE (p. 200). If, however, the paper is being submitted to a journal for possible publication, the entries should be double-spaced both within the entry and between the entries, as they are in these models.

(1) A single book by a single author:

```
Seki, Hozen. The Great Natural Way. New York:
    American Buddhist Academy, 1976.
Landon, John W. Jesse Crawford: Poet of the
    Organ, Wizard of the Mighty Wurlitzer. Ves-
    tal, NY: The Vestal Press, 1974.
```

(2) A single book by more than one author:

```
Baran, Paul A., and Paul M. Sweezy. Monopoly
    Capital: An Essay on American Economic and
    Social Order. New York: Monthly Review
    Press, 1966.
```

(Only the name of the first author should be inverted. Notice that the subtitle, which was omitted in the footnote, is included here.)

(3) A book of more than one volume:

```
Hays, William Lee, and Robert L. Winkler. Sta-
    tistics: Probability, Inference, and Deci-
```

```
sion. 2 vols. New York: Holt, Rinehart &
Winston, 1970.
```

(4) A book edited by one or more editors:

```
Essays in American Economic History. Ed.
    Alfred W. Coats and Ross M. Robertson. Lon-
    don: Edward Arnold, 1969.
The Letters of Jonathan Swift to Charles Ford.
    Ed. David Nichol Smith. Oxford: Clarendon
    Press, 1935.
```

*(In the bibliography, these books would be filed alphabetically according to the first significant word in the title—***Essays** *and* **Letters** *respectively.)*

(5) An essay or a chapter by an author in an edited collection:

```
Svaglic, Martin J. "Classical Rhetoric and Vic-
    torian Prose." The Art of Victorian Prose.
    Ed. George Levine and William Madden. New
    York: Oxford Univ. Press, 1968, pp. 268-88.
```

(Because this essay is part of a collection, the full span of pages is cited in the bibliography.)

(6) A new edition of a book:

Format of the Research Paper

> Doughty, Oswald. A Victorian Romantic, Dante
> Gabriel Rossetti. 2nd ed. London: Oxford
> Univ. Press, 1960.

(7) A book that is part of a series:

> Heytesbury, William. Medieval Logic and the
> Rise of Mathematical Physics. University of
> Wisconsin Publications in Medieval Science,
> No. 3. Madison: Univ. of Wisconsin Press,
> 1956.

(8) A book in a paperback series:

> Wilson, Edmund. To the Finland Station. Anchor
> Books. Garden City, NY: Doubleday, 1955.

(9) A translation:

> Dostoevsky, Fyodor. Crime and Punishment.
> Trans. Constance Garnett. New York: Herit-
> age Press, 1938.
> Ellul, Jacques. A Critique of the New Common-
> places. Trans. Helen Weaver. New York:
> Knopf, 1968.

(10) A signed and an unsigned article from an encyclopedia:

```
Ewing, J. A. "Steam-Engine and Other Heat-
     Engines." Encyclopaedia Britannica. 9th ed.,
     XXII, 473-526.
"Dwarfed Trees." Encyclopedia Americana. 1948,
     IX, 445-46.
```

(Notice that the full span of pages of these articles is given.)

(11) An article from a journal:

```
Adkins, Nelson. "Emerson and the Bardic Tradi-
     tion." Publications of the Modern Language
     Association, 72 (1948), 662-7.
Windt, Theodore Otto, Jr. "The Diatribe: Last
     Resort for Protest." Quarterly Journal of
     Speech, 58 (1972), 1-14.
```

(Although in footnotes well-known scholarly journals are commonly referred to by their abbreviated title, it is advisable to give the full title in the bibliography.)

Format of the Research Paper

(12) An article in a popular magazine:

```
Levin, Robert J. "Sex, Morality, and Society."
    Saturday Review, 9 July 1966, pp. 29-30.
Silberman, Charles E. "Technology Is Knocking
    on the Schoolhouse Door." Fortune, Aug.
    1966, pp. 120-25.
```

(13) A signed and an unsigned article in a newspaper:

```
Gilman, Art. "Altering U. S. Flag for Political
    Causes Stirs a Legal Debate." Wall Street
    Journal, 12 June 1970, p. 1.
"Twin Games Bid: Wrestling, Judo." New York
    Times, 9 April 1972, Section 5, p. 15,
    cols. 4-6.
```

(14) A signed book review:

```
Dalbor, John B. Review of Meaning and Mind: A
    Study in the Psychology of Language, by
    Robert F. Terwilliger. Philosophy & Rheto-
    ric, 5 (1972), 60-61.
Gill, Brendan. Review of Ibsen, by Michael
    Meyer. New Yorker, 8 April 1972, pp. 126-
    30.
```

Format of the Research Paper: Model Research Paper (with footnotes at bottom of page)

A Study of the Various Interpretations
of
"Young Goodman Brown"

Diana Lynn Ikenberry
English 302
January 7, 1977

Format of the Research Paper

A Study of the Various Interpretations
of
"Young Goodman Brown"

Nathaniel Hawthorne's "Young Goodman Brown" has been
subjected to various interpretations. A prime reason for so
many different interpretations is the story's extremely ambiguous nature. One critic seldom agrees with another as to
why various parts of the story are ambiguous. One question
that has engaged many critics is whether Goodman Brown actually went into the forest and met the devil or whether he
only dreamed that he did. Richard Fogle is one critic who
believes that Hawthorne failed to answer this question defin-
itively, because "the ambiguities of meaning are intentional,
an integral part of his purpose."[1] Fogle feels that the
ambiguity results from unanswered questions like the one
above. And it is just this ambiguity or "device of multiple
choice,"[2] as Fogle calls it, that is the very essence of
"Young Goodman Brown."

Critic Thomas F. Walsh, Jr. went a step further in
analyzing the ambiguity of Brown's journey into the forest.[3]
He agreed with Fogle that the reader can never be certain
whether the journey was real or imaginary; however, the

---

[1] Richard H. Fogle, "Ambiguity and Clarity in Hawthorne's
'Young Goodman Brown,'" New England Quarterly, 18 (December,
1945), 448.

[2] Ibid., p. 449.

[3] Thomas F. Walsh, Jr., "The Bedeviling of Young Goodman
Brown," Modern Language Quarterly, 19 (December, 1958), 331-6.

reader can be certain "not only of the nature and stages of
Goodman Brown's despair, but also of its probable cause."[4]
Walsh also points out that the effect upon Brown, once he
emerges from the forest, is quite clear: "Goodman Brown
lived and died an unhappy, despairing man."[5] It is Walsh's
view that the only solution to the problem of ambiguity in
relation to what happened in the forest can be found in the
story's complex symbolic pattern.

D. M. McKeithan's view of Brown's journey is unlike
any of the previously mentioned views. He feels that, in
reality, Goodman Brown neither journeyed into the forest
that night nor dreamed that he did. What Brown did do,
according to McKeithan, was "to indulge in sin (represented
by the journey into the forest that night . . .)," thinking
that he could break away from his sinfulness whenever he
chose to.[6] However, Brown indulged in sin longer than he
expected and "suffered the consequences, which were the loss
of religious faith and faith in all other human beings."[7]

All of these critics have something to add to readers'
notions about the ambiguous nature of "Young Goodman Brown."
It is the purpose of this paper to study some of these critics'
interpretations, as well as the interpretations of some critics

---

[4] Ibid., p. 332.

[5] Walsh, p. 336.

[6] D. M. McKeithan, "Hawthorne's 'Young Goodman Brown': An
Interpretation," _Modern Language Notes_, 67 (February, 1952), 96.

[7] Ibid.

Format of the Research Paper

not yet mentioned, to see just exactly what they have to add to the interpretation of Hawthorne's masterpiece. I will focus primarily on two areas of interpretations: the realizations of Goodman Brown's faith and the over-all implications of the story itself. These two areas proved to be quite controversial.

Despite all the ambiguities of meaning mentioned above, I must conclude that young Goodman Brown did come to some realizations about his own personal faith. When Brown starts out on his journey into the forest, he is confident that his faith will carry him to heaven. As Thomas E. Connolly points out, "it is in this concept that his disillusionment will come."[8] I must agree with Connolly's statement, for Brown thinks that his wife delayed his journey, but when he arrives at the meeting place with the devil, his Faith is already there. Brown's confidence in his virtuous wife has been shattered, and from this point on, he cannot be at peace with himself nor with any of those around him.

Not only does Connolly suggest Brown's disillusionment, but he argues that Brown's Calvinistic religion is a major cause of his disillusionment.[9] Connolly presents this doctrine of Calvinism to his readers:

> Calvinism teaches that man is innately depraved and that he can do nothing to merit

---

[8] Thomas E. Connolly, "Hawthorne's 'Young Goodman Brown': An Attack on Puritanic Calvinism," _American Literature_, 28 (November, 1956), 372.

[9] Ibid., p. 375.

Model Research Paper

> salvation. He is saved only by the whim
> of God who selects some, through no de-
> serts of their own, for heaven while the
> great mass of mankind is destined for hell.[10]

I think Goodman Brown was a Calvinist, in the sense that he
believed himself to be one of God's Elect. I do not think,
however, that Brown found nothing to merit salvation, for
even though he believed himself to be one of the Elect, he
knew he must cling to his faith in order to get to heaven.
One particular group of Calvinists, known as Antinomians,[11]
were quite active during the time Hawthorne was writing "Young
Goodman Brown." It seems quite possible that this Calvinistic
group could have influenced Hawthorne's characterizations.
The Antinomians insisted that salvation was a function of
faith, for even a man's good works were secondary to his faith.
This "mysterious divine grace,"[12] as James W. Mathews calls it,
"was contingent on the degree of the individual's faith,"[13]
while a strong faith was a good indication of predestined
salvation. Extreme Antinomians believed that a man who was
of God's Elect could be confident of salvation, no matter
how the man conducted himself in his daily living. It seems
quite possible, then, that Brown could be classified as an
Antinomian, since he was depending on his faith to carry him

---

[10] Ibid., p. 374.

[11] James W. Mathews, "Antinomianism in 'Young Goodman
Brown,'" Studies in Short Fiction, 3 (Fall, 1965), 73-5.

[12] Mathews, p. 73.

[13] Ibid.

Format of the Research Paper

to heaven.

Mathews makes a strong case for Hawthorne's development of Antinomianism within young Goodman Brown. Brown himself does stress the theoretical rather than the practical side of his religion, as does the Antinomian doctrine. Brown states at one point in the story that "we are a people of prayer, and good works to boot, and abide no such wickedness."[14] Later in the story, Brown further adds, "With heaven above and Faith below, I will yet stand firm against the devil!" (p. 15). He is quite confident that his being one of God's Elect, along with his having Faith at home, will prevent any of the night's evil doings from becoming obstacles in his path to salvation.

It seems important at this point to look at Faith's relationship with her husband. Brown knows that his journey is of a sinful nature: "Poor little Faith! . . . What a wretch am I to leave her on such an errand!" (p. 10). Brown clearly manifests a sense of guilt for leaving his wife, because he seems to think it would "kill her" if she knew why he was going on his journey. However, I think Faith does know his purpose, because she says to her husband,

---

[14] This and subsequent quotations from the story "Young Goodman Brown" are taken from the text of the story as reprinted in Nathaniel Hawthorne: Young Goodman Brown, ed. Thomas E. Connolly (Columbus, Ohio: Charles E. Merrill Publishing Company, 1968), pp. 10-21. Hereafter, quotations from this version of the story will be documented with page-numbers in parentheses at the end of the quotation.

Model Research Paper

> "Dearest heart," whispered she, softly
> and rather sadly . . . "prithee put off
> your journey until sunrise and sleep in
> your own bed tonight. . . . Pray tarry
> with me this night, dear husband, of all
> nights in the year" (p. 10).

Why would Faith be <u>sad</u> to see her husband leave for just
one night, and why would she <u>beg</u> him to stay home on this
particular evening? Faith not only realizes her husband's
plans but even gives her consent and asks for God's blessing
to be with Brown when he insists that he must go: "'Then God
bless you!' said Faith, . . . 'and may you find all well
when you come back'" (p. 10). I think Faith is particularly
concerned with her husband's state of mind <u>after</u> the night's
experience. Faith does not appear extremely worried about
his leaving, but I think she doubts whether he can accept the
consequences. Faith's ability to see that her husband may
suffer from the results of his journey is Hawthorne's way of
subtly informing his readers that Faith is the wiser and the
more realistic of the two. She knows that her husband will
soon find out the hard way that Faith--both his wife <u>and</u> his
religion--cannot be used at his convenience whenever he is
troubled.

Connolly sheds an even brighter light upon young
Goodman Brown's faith. He points out that Brown did not
lose his faith at all. What Brown did do was not only retain his faith but actually discover "the full and frightening
significance of his faith."[15] Connolly illustrates his point

---

[15] Connolly, p. 371.

193

Format of the Research Paper

with this line from the story: "And when he had lived long, and was borne to his grave a hoary corpse, followed by Faith, an aged woman, and children and grandchildren, . . . they carved no hopeful verse upon his tombstone, for his dying hour was gloom" (p. 21). I must agree with Connolly that Brown's faith--both his wife and his religion--did survive him. Brown did not lose his wife, even though he did lose the love and trust that had once linked them together happily. And Brown did not lose his religion, for I feel that when Hawthorne wrote this story, he knew that the Calvinistic faith would outlive Goodman Brown. I think Hawthorne realizes that many more "young Goodman Browns" would perish as an indirect result of such a dehumanizing religion.

Besides the subject of faith in "Young Goodman Brown," I would also like to touch upon the over-all implications of the story. Without a doubt, ambiguity is quite prevalent throughout the story. For example, one critic asked, "Does the story have universal significance, or is it merely an individual tragedy?"[16] Another critic questioned whether young Goodman Brown represents the majority of the human race or only a small segment of the human population.[17] Various critics have asked similar questions and have

---

[16] Paul W. Miller, "Hawthorne's 'Young Goodman Brown': Cynicism or Meliorism?" Nineteenth-Century Fiction, 14 (December, 1959), 255.

[17] Ibid.

arrived at a variety of answers.

Paul W. Miller is one critic who has struggled with the question of whether Brown should be viewed as an individual or a type, representing either all of mankind or only a segment of it. Miller seems to think that no conclusion can be drawn concerning Brown's representation because the answer depends on "one's understanding of Hawthorne's view of man when he wrote the story, as well as one's interpretation of this enigmatic but nonetheless fascinating tale."[18] Miller contends that if young Goodman Brown is intended to represent all mankind, then Hawthorne must be regarded as a totally cynical man; whereas if Brown represents only a segment of mankind, then Hawthorne could be viewed less pessimistically. Miller brings up an interesting point here. If Brown does not represent all mankind, are men like Brown doomed by their nature alone to be separated from God, or does the society in which they live play a major role in separating them from God?[19] I think that, in Brown's case, the society in which he lives has developed a religion that refuses to acknowledge sin as an inevitable human weakness. Man is responsible for his separation from God, but the Calvinistic religion seems to suggest that a man's reunification with God is unobtainable if he is not one of the

---

[18] Ibid.

[19] Miller, p. 256.

Format of the Research Paper

Elect. Human society ultimately strives to develop a religion to fill man's need for spiritual comfort, but it appears that the Calvinists developed a religion that tortured man's spirit. What portion of mankind, then, does Brown represent? Miller contends that

> he represents those weaker members of a
> puritanical society who are traumatized,
> arrested in their spiritual development,
> and finally destroyed by the discovery
> that their society is full of "whited
> sepulchres."[20]

I find Miller's interpretation more acceptable than other critics' views. Young Goodman Brown's spiritual development has been not only retarded but warped at the same time, but I do not think Brown himself can be fully blamed.

I can agree only in part with D. M. McKeithan's opinion about the over-all implication of the story.[21] He contends that

> this is not a story of the disillusionment
> that comes to a person when he discovers
> that many supposedly religious and vir-
> tuous people are really sinful; it is,
> rather, a story of a man whose sin led
> him to consider all other people sinful.[22]

I think Brown is extremely disillusioned when he realizes the sinful nature of Goody Cloyse, Deacon Gookin, and his own wife, Faith. As I view the story, this disillusionment, which denies all that Brown had previously believed, is a major factor in

---

[20] Ibid., p. 262.

[21] McKeithan, pp. 93-6.

[22] Ibid., pp. 95-6.

-10-

the over-all meaning of the story. Those persons who had always seemed virtuous, pure, and representative of Brown's religion were suddenly seen in a different light--a definite disillusionment for young Goodman Brown. Contrary to McKeithan's view, the story does seem to imply that Brown is disillusioned when he discovers that certain virtuous people are sinful and that Brown becomes painfully aware of his own sinfulness and of the sinfulness of his fellowmen. However, even with the disillusionment that Brown faces and the realization of his own sinful nature, he still fails to perceive two very important characteristics of sin: its universal and inevitable nature.

I also agree, in part, with Herbert Schneider, who places particular importance on Hawthorne's concern with the sinful side of human nature. He writes of Hawthorne,

> For him sin is an obvious and conspicuous fact, to deny which is foolish. Its consequences are inevitable and to seek escape from them is childish. The only relief from sin comes from public confession. Anything private or concealed works internally until it destroys the sinner's soul.[23]

I strongly agree with Schneider that Hawthorne's denial of sin is foolish and that its consequences are inevitable. However, I question whether Hawthorne feels that a <u>public</u> confession is the sole relief from sin. I think Hawthorne would feel that a private confession could adequately render

---

[23] Herbert W. Schneider, <u>The Puritan Mind</u> (New York: H. Holt and Company, 1930), p. 260.

Format of the Research Paper

a sense of relief from one's sinfulness. Young Goodman Brown was unable to bring himself to make either a public or a private confession. He could not accept the sin he saw in others nor the sin present within himself, primarily because Calvinistic teachings failed to inform him that sin in man is inevitable. Paul Miller sums up my feelings quite well when he says,

> In "Young Goodman Brown," then, Hawthorne
> . . . is pleading that what survives of
> Puritan rigorism in society be sloughed off
> and replaced by a striving for virtue start-
> ing from the confession of common human
> weakness. Such a society would be based
> upon the firm foundation of humility and
> honesty rather than the sinking sands of
> human pride and the hypocrisy that accom-
> panies it.[24]

I do agree with Miller that even a type like Brown could survive in a society like the one described above. Society can truly have an adverse effect upon man, as did Goodman Brown's society. But, at the same time, man must face the realities of society, as Faith seemed to do, even though the pressures of society oftentimes seem unbearable.

Doesn't it seem slightly odd that the mere actions of one character could elicit so many interpretations from critics? That there should be so many different interpretations seems quite out of the ordinary to me. Yet when one considers the questions that Nathaniel Hawthorne was dealing with in "Young Goodman Brown," the ambiguity present in the story seems as

---

[24] Miller, p. 264.

inevitable as the sin that is present in man. In "Young
Goodman Brown," Hawthorne found himself dealing with the
mysteries about human nature and the human mind, two mysteries that naturally stimulate man to question. And this
questioning will go on forever, hopefully, because unless
man finds answers to questions concerning his spiritual
being or to questions concerning all the intricacies of
the human mind, life will hardly be worth living.

I think Hawthorne truly valued this questioning when he
wrote this masterpiece. By his dealing with man's faith and
man's society, Hawthorne was able to stimulate man to question
his beliefs and his own personal role in society. Hawthorne
wanted to point out to the Calvinists in a subtle way that
their religious teachings were having an adverse effect upon
certain people. And I think he wanted the Calvinists to see
that the society--not the individual--needed the reform.
Through his characterization of Faith, Hawthorne was able to
show that man could be considered virtuous, even though he
is guilty of some degree of sin. And, finally, I think
Hawthorne wanted his readers to see that man's doubtfulness
concerning his salvation was _natural_ and _necessary_, for if man
definitely knew that he was one of God's Elect, he would take
love and faith and peace of mind for granted. Young Goodman
Brown lost all doubt concerning his salvation for only one
night, but his experience on that one night caused Brown to
live the rest of his life as an extremely unhappy man.

Format of the Research Paper

BIBLIOGRAPHY

Connolly, Thomas E. "Hawthorne's 'Young Goodman Brown': An Attack on Puritanic Calvinism," _American Literature_, 28 (November, 1956), 370-5.

Fogle, Richard H. "Ambiguity and Clarity in Hawthorne's 'Young Goodman Brown,'" _New England Quarterly_, 18 (December, 1945), 448-465.

Hawthorne, Nathaniel. "Young Goodman Brown," _Nathaniel Hawthorne: Young Goodman Brown_, ed. Thomas E. Connolly. Columbus, Ohio: Charles E. Merrill Publishing Company, 1968, pp. 10-21.

McKeithan, D. M. "Hawthorne's 'Young Goodman Brown': An Interpretation," _Modern Language Notes_, 67 (February, 1952), 93-6.

Mathews, James W. "Antinomianism in 'Young Goodman Brown,'" _Studies in Short Fiction_, 3 (Fall, 1965), 73-5.

Miller, Paul W. "Hawthorne's 'Young Goodman Brown': Cynicism or Meliorism?" _Nineteenth-Century Fiction_, 14 (December, 1959), 255-264.

Schneider, Herbert W. _The Puritan Mind_. New York: Henry Holt and Company, 1930.

Walsh, Thomas F., Jr. "The Bedeviling of Young Goodman Brown," _Modern Language Quarterly_, 19 (December, 1958), 331-6.

(The bibliography for a paper submitted as a classroom assignment may be single-spaced, as it is in the model above. The bibliography for a paper submitted for publication, however, should be double-spaced, both within the entry and between entries, as in the MODELS FOR BIBLIOGRAPHY _[pp. 181–186]. Notice that the entries above are arranged in alphabetical order.)_

(O)
Format of the Research Paper:
Model for Footnotes Entered on Separate Pages

If footnotes are entered on separate pages at the end of a research paper submitted as a classroom assignment, they may be single-spaced within the footnote and double-spaced between footnotes, just as they are at the bottom of the page in the sample pages of the research paper. If a paper is submitted for publication, however, the footnotes must be entered on separate pages and must be double-spaced both within and between footnotes, as they are in the model below.

[1]All my quotations from the "Elegy" are taken from the final approved version of 1753, as printed in Herbert W. Starr and John R. Hendrickson, eds., The Complete Poems of Thomas Gray, English, Latin, and Greek (Oxford: Clarendon Press, 1966). Hereafter, quotations from this edition of the poem will be documented by line numbers in parentheses.

[2]Samuel Johnson, "Gray," The Lives of the English Poets, ed. George Birkbeck Hill (Oxford: Clarendon Press, 1905), III, 442.

[3]Odell Shephard, "A Youth to Fortune and to Fame Unknown," _Modern Philology_, 20 (1923), 347-73.

[4]_Ibid._, p. 348.

[5]A detailed description of the various manuscript versions is given in Francis G. Stokes, ed., _An Elegy Written in a Country Churchyard_ (Oxford: Clarendon Press, 1929), pp. 23-6. Herbert W. Starr has also presented an illuminating study of the successive versions of the poem in his article "Gray's Craftsmanship," _JEGP_, 45 (1946), 415-29.

[6]Shephard, p. 366.

[7]_Ibid._, pp. 371-72.

[8]H. W. Starr, "'A Youth to Fortune and to Fame Unknown': A Re-estimation," _JEGP_, 48 (1949), 97-107.

Format of the Research Paper:
The APA System of Documentation

If the MLA system of documentation, illustrated in the previous section, is predominant in the humanities, the American Psychological Association (APA) system is predominant in such fields as psychology, education, psycholinguistics, and many of the social sciences. Over a hundred scholarly journals in the United States now prescribe the APA style of documentation. The highlights of this system will be presented here; for a fuller treatment, consult the readily available paperback edition of *Publication Manual of the American Psychological Association*, 2nd ed. (Washington, D. C.: American Psychological Association, 1974).

The two principal differences between the MLA and the APA systems are as follows:

(1) Whereas the MLA system documents quotations and other kinds of references in footnotes printed either at the bottom of the page or on separate pages, the APA system documents all citations *within parentheses in the text*.

(2) Whereas the MLA system supplies complete bibliographic information about a work the first time that work is cited in a footnote, the APA system supplies only the *last name of the author,* the *publication date of the work*, and sometimes the *page number*.

Here is how the first reference to a book would be documented, first in the MLA style and then in the APA style:

Format of the Research Paper

[3]Mina P. Shaughnessy, <u>Errors</u> <u>and</u> <u>Expecta-</u>
<u>tions</u>: <u>A</u> <u>Guide</u> <u>for</u> <u>the</u> <u>Teacher</u> <u>of</u> <u>Basic</u> <u>Writing</u>
(New York: Oxford University Press, 1977),
p. 57.

(Shaughnessy, 1977, p. 57).

Readers who wanted fuller information about the work cited in the parenthetical reference could turn to the list of references at the end of the paper. There, in an alphabetical listing, the Shaughnessy work would be entered in double-spaced typescript as follows:

Shaughnessy, M. P. <u>Errors</u> <u>and</u> <u>expectations</u>: <u>A</u>

   <u>guide</u> <u>for</u> <u>the</u> <u>teacher</u> <u>of</u> <u>basic</u> <u>writing</u>. New

   York: Oxford University Press, 1977.

VARIATIONS ON THE BASIC APA STYLE OF DOCUMENTATION

(a)   If a whole work is being referred to, only the author's last name and the date of the work are given in parentheses.

A recent study has confirmed that twelve-year-
olds grow at an amazingly rapid rate (Swanson,
1969).

(b) A page number or a chapter number is supplied only if part of a work is being referred to. Quotations always demand the addition of a page number.

```
The committee boldly declared that "morality
could not be enforced, but it could be bought"
(Dawson, 1975, p. 105).
```

(c) Any information supplied in the text itself need not be repeated in the parentheses.

```
Anderson (1948) found that only middle-class
Europeans disdained our cultural values.

In 1965, Miller professed his fervent admira-
tion of our admissions policy.
```

(d) If a work has two authors, both authors should be cited each time a reference is made to that text. If a work has three or more authors, all the authors should be cited the first time, but subsequently only the name of the first author followed by **et al.** needs to be given.

```
The circulation of false rumors poisoned the
environment of that conference (Getty & Howard,
1979).
```

Format of the Research Paper

> The overall effect of the smear tactics was a
> marked decline in voter registrations (Abraham,
> Davis & Keppler, 1952).
>
> In three successive national elections, voters
> from Slavic neighborhoods showed a 72% turnout
> (Abraham et al., 1952, pp. 324-327).

(e) If several works are cited at the same point in the text, the works should be arranged alphabetically according to the last name of the author and should be separated with semi-colons.

> All the studies of the problem agree that the
> proposed remedy is worse than the malady (Brown
> & Turkell, 1964; Firkins, 1960; Howells, 1949;
> Jackson, Miller, & Naylor, undated; Kameron,
> in press).

(f) If several works by the same author are cited in the same reference, the works are distinguished by the publication dates, arranged in chronological·order and separated with commas. Two or more works published by the same author in the same year are distinguished by the letters **a, b, c,** etc., added to the repeated date. In such chronological listings, works "in press" are always listed last.

> A consistent view on this point has been re-
> peatedly expressed by the Canadian member of
> the Commission (Holden, 1959, 1965, 1970, 1971a,
> 1971b, 1976).

(g) If no author is given for a work, two or three words from another part of the entry (usually from the title) should be used to refer to the work.

> The voters' apathy was decried in the final
> spring meeting of the city council ("The
> Gradual Decline," 1976).

LIST OF REFERENCES

The *References* page appended to a paper that observes the APA style is comparable to, and yet different from, the *Bibliography* page in a paper that observes the MLA style. Both systems give full bibliographic information about the works cited in the body of the writing, and both systems arrange the entries alphabetically according to the last name of the author. In both systems, the names of the authors are inverted (surname first), but in the APA system, only the initials of first and middle names are given, and when there are two or more authors for a work, the names of *all* the authors are inverted.

The conventions of sequence, punctuation, and capitalization in the APA style for the *References* section can most easily be illustrated with examples.

Format of the Research Paper

(1) A book by a single author:

```
Luria, A. R.  The working brain: An introduct-
    ion to neuro-psychology. London: Penguin,
    1973.
```

Note that the title of the book is underlined but that only the first word of the title and the first word following the colon in the title are capitalized. (Any proper nouns in a title would also be capitalized; see the following example.) The three main parts of an entry—author, title, and publication data—are separated with periods.

(2) A book by several authors:

```
Koslin, S., Koslin, B.L., Pargament, R., &
    Pendelton, S.  An evaluation of fifth grade
    reading programs in ten New York City Com-
    munity School Districts, 1973-1974.  New
    York: Riverside Research Institute, 1975.
```

Note that the names of all the authors are inverted, that the names are separated with commas, and that an ampersand (**&**) is put before the last name in the series (even when there are only two names; see the following example.)

(3) An article in an edited collection:

```
Bobrow, D. G., & Norman, D. A. Some principles
    of memory schemata.  In D. G. Bobrow & A. M.
    Collins (Eds.), Representation and under-
    standing: Studies in cognitive science.  New
    York: Academic Press, 1975.
```

Note that the title of the article (**Some principles** etc.) is not enclosed in quotation marks and that only the first word of this title is capitalized. (Any proper nouns in the title of the article would, of course, be capitalized.) Note also that the subsequent names of the two editors (**Eds.**) of the collection are not inverted and that there is no comma between the names.

(4) An article in a journal:

```
Stahl, A.  The structure of children's composi-
    tions: Developmental and ethnic differences.
    Research in the Teaching of English, 1977,
    11, 156-163.
```

Note that all substantive words in the title of the journal are capitalized and that the title of the journal is underlined. Note also that the year comes before the volume number and that the volume number (**11**) is underlined. For a journal that begins the numbering of its pages with page 1 in each issue, the number of the issue should be indicated with an Arabic number following the volume number—**11(3)**.

Format of the Research Paper

(5) A book by a corporate author:

American Psychological Association. <u>Standards</u>
<u>for</u> <u>educational</u> <u>and</u> <u>psychological</u> <u>tests</u> <u>and</u>
<u>manuals</u>. Washington, DC: Author, 1966.

Books and articles with corporate authors are listed alphabetically according to the first significant word of the entry (here **American**). The word **Author** listed with the publication data indicates that the publisher of the work is the same as the group named in the author slot. If, however, the publisher is different from the corporate author, the name of that publisher would be given right after the place of publication.

These five models cover most of the kinds of published material likely to be used in a research paper. For additional models, consult the *Publication Manual of the American Psychological Association* (2nd ed.).

For an illustration of the physical appearance, in typescript, of a research paper and of a *References* page done according to the APA system of documentation, see the following pages, taken from a twenty-one-page article by Carl Bereiter of the Ontario Institute for Studies in Education: "Development in Writing," in *Testing, Teaching and Learning* (Washington, D. C.: National Institute of Education, 1979), pp. 146-166. This article was later reprinted in its entirety in L. W. Gregg and E. R. Steinberg, eds., *Cognitive Processes in Writing* (Hillsdale, N. J.: Erlbaum, 1979).

DEVELOPMENT IN WRITING

Carl Bereiter

Although there is a substantial body of data on the development of writing skills, it has not seemed to have much implication for instruction. Reviews of writing research from an educational perspective have given scant attention to it (Blount, 1973; Braddock, Lloyd-Jones, & Schoer, 1963; Lyman, 1929; West, 1967). Generally speaking, developmental research has educational significance only when there is a conceptual apparatus linking it with questions of practical significance.

Almost all of the data on writing development consist of frequency counts--words per communication unit, incidence of different kinds of dependent clauses, frequency of different types of writing at different ages, and so on. The conceptual frameworks used for interpreting these data have come largely from linguistics (e.g., Hunt, 1965; Loban, 1976; O'Donnell, Griffin, & Norris, 1967). However informative these analyses might be to the student of language development, they are disappointing from an educational point of view. The variables they look at seem unrelated to commonly held purposes of writing instruction (Nystrand, 1977).

The purpose of this paper is to synthesize findings on the growth of writing skills within what may be called an "applied cognitive-developmental" framework. Key issues within an applied cognitive-developmental framework are the cognitive strategies children use and how these are adapted to their limited information processing capacities (Case, 1975, 1978; Klahr & Wallace, 1976; Scardamalia, in press). Although this paper will not deal with instructional implications, it will become evident that the issues considered within an applied cognitive-

Format of the Research Paper

developmental framework are relevant to such concerns of writing instruction as fluency, coherence, correctness, sense of audience, style, and thought content.

What Is Development in Writing?

Students' writing will undoubtedly reflect their overall language development (Loban, 1976; O'Donnell et al., 1967) and also their level of cognitive development (Collis & Biggs, undated; Scardamalia, in press). It is to be expected that it will also at times reflect their level of moral development, social cognition, etc. Given the small role that writing plays in most children's lives, it is therefore reasonable to suppose that there is no such thing as writing development as such--that it is merely the resultant of other, more basic kinds of development. This view is implicit in the speech-primacy position of researchers like Loban (1963, 1966, 1976), who treat children's writing simply as another source of data on their language development.

While it may be reasonable to treat writing development as a reflection of other kinds of development, it is not very useful to do so. An educationally relevant account of writing development would have to give prominence to whatever is distinctive about writing and potentially susceptible to direct influence. The following have been recognized as distinctive characteristics of writing.

1. Written English may be recognized as a subsystem of English, along with spoken English, and distinguishable from the latter in a number of ways. It is usually more compact, contains more elaborately specified subjects, and shows less local variation than spoken English, and generally shows a different distribution of linguistic devices and usages (Allen, 1972; Gleason, 1965; Long, 1961).

2. Written English and spoken English are predominately, but not

APA-Style Research Paper

References

Allen, R. L. English grammars and English grammar. New York: Scribner's,
   1972.

Blount, N. S. Research on teaching literature, language, and composition.
   In R. M. W. Travers (Ed.), Second handbook of research on teaching.
   Chicago: Rand-McNally, 1973.

Braddock, R., Lloyd-Jones, R., & Schoer, L. Research in written composition. Champaign, IL: National Council of Teachers of English, 1963.

Case, R. Gearing the demands of instruction to the developmental capacities of the learner. Review of Educational Research, 1975, 45(1),
   59-87.

Case, R. Implications of developmental psychology for the design of
   effective instruction. In A. M. Lesgold, J. W. Pellegrino, S. D.
   Fokemma, & R. Glaser (Eds.), Cognitive psychology and instruction.
   Plenum, NY: Division of Plenum Publishing Corporation, 1978.

Collis, K. F., & Biggs, J. B. Classroom examples of cognitive development phenomena. ERDC Funded Project 7/41, University of Newcastle,
   undated.

Gleason, H. A., Jr. Linguistics and English grammar. New York: Holt,
   Rinehart & Winston, 1965.

Hunt, K. W. Grammatical structures written at three grade levels.
   Champaign, IL: National Council of Teachers of English, 1965.
   (Research Report No. 3.)

Klahr, D., & Wallace, J. G. Cognitive development: An information-
   processing view. Hillsdale, NJ: Erlbaum, 1976.

Format of the Research Paper

Loban, W. The language of elementary school children. Urbana, IL:
    National Council of Teachers of English, 1963. (Research Report No. 1.)

Loban, W. Problems in oral English. Urbana, IL: National Council
    of Teachers of English, 1966. (Research Report No. 5.)

Loban, W. Language development: Kindergarten through grade twelve.
    Urbana, IL: National Council of Teachers of English, 1976. (Research
    Report No. 18.)

Long, R. B. The sentence and its parts: A grammar of contemporary
    English. Chicago: University of Chicago Press, 1961.

Lyman, R. Summary of investigations relating to grammar, language, and
    composition. Chicago: University of Chicago, 1929. (Supplementary
    educational Monographs, No. 36, published in conjunction with
    The School Review and The Elementary School Journal.)

Nystrand, M. Assessing written communication competence: A textual
    cognition model. Toronto, Canada: The Ontario Institute for
    Studies in Education, 1977. (ERIC Document Reproduction Service
    No. ED 133 732.)

O'Donnell, R. C., Griffin, W. J., & Norris, R. C. Syntax of kinder-
    garten and elementary school children: A transformational analysis.
    Champaign, IL: National Council of Teachers of English, 1967.
    (Research Report No. 8.)

Scardamalia, M. How children cope with the cognitive demands of
    writing. In C. H. Frederiksen, M. S. Whiteman, & J. F. Dominic (Eds.),
    Writing: The nature, development, and teaching of written communi-
    cation, in press.

West, W. W. Written composition. Review of Educational Research, 1967,
    37(2), 159-167.

Forms For Letters

General Instructions

The one type of writing that most people engage in after they leave school is letter-writing. They will almost certainly write letters to parents, friends, and acquaintances, and they may have to write letters in connection with their jobs. Occasionally, they may feel compelled to write a letter to the editor of a newspaper or magazine, and sometimes, they may write more formal letters to institutions or officials for such purposes as applying for a job, requesting information or service, or seeking redress of some grievance. Although they do not have to be much concerned about the niceties of form when they are writing to intimate friends, they would be well advised to observe the conventions of form and etiquette in letters addressed to people that they do not know well enough to call by their first names.

FORMAT OF FAMILIAR LETTER

Letters written to acquaintances are commonly referred to as *familiar letters*. Although usually "anything goes" in letters to

Forms for Letters

acquaintances, one should keep in mind that even the most intimate acquaintance is flattered if the author of the letter observes certain amenities of form. Here is a list of the conventions for the familiar letter:

(a) Familiar letters may be written on lined or unlined paper of any size, but usually they are written on note-size stationery of some pastel color.

(b) Familiar letters may be handwritten and may be written on both sides of the sheet of paper.

(c) The author of the letter usually puts his or her address and the date at the right-hand side of the heading but does not, as in a business letter, put at the left-hand side of the heading the name and address of the person to whom the letter is addressed.

(d) Depending on the degree of intimacy with the addressee, the writer may use salutations like these: **Dear Mom, Dear Jim, Dear Julie, Dear Ms. Worth**. The salutation is often followed by a comma rather than the more formal colon.

(e) The body of the letter may be written in indented paragraphs, single- or double-spaced.

(f) Depending on the degree of intimacy with the addressee, the writer may use complimentary closes like these: **Sincerely, Cordially, Affectionately, Yours, Much love, Fondly, As ever**.

(g) Depending on the degree of intimacy with the addressee, the writer may sign his or her full name or just a first name or a nickname.

FORMAT OF BUSINESS LETTER

Formal letters addressed to organizations or strangers or superiors are commonly called *business letters*. The form of business letters is more strictly prescribed than the form of familiar letters. Models for a business letter appear on pp. (219) and (221). Here is a list of the conventions for the business letter:

(a)   Business letters are written on 8½ × 11 unlined paper or on 8½ × 11 paper with a printed letterhead.

(b)   Business letters must be typewritten, single-spaced, on one side of the paper only.

(c)   In the sample business letter that is typed on printed letterhead stationery (p. 221), the so-called *full block* format of formal business letters is illustrated. Note that in this format, everything—date, address, greeting, text, salutation, etc.—begins at the left-hand margin. Compare this format with the *semiblock* format of the sample business letter that is typed on plain white paper (p. 219). All the other directions about format (**d, e, f, g, h, i, j**) apply to both kinds of formal business letters.

(d)   Flush with the left-hand margin and in single-spaced block form, the writer should type the name and address of the person or the organization to whom the letter is written. (The same form will be used in addressing the envelope.)

(e)   Two spaces below this inside address and flush with the left-hand margin, the writer should type the salutation, followed by a colon. In addressing an organization rather than a specific person in that organization, the writer can use salutations like **Dear Sir** or **Gentlemen** or **Dear Madam** or **Ladies**. If the writer knows the name of the person, he or she should use the last name, prefaced with **Mr.** or **Miss** or **Mrs.** or, if uncertain about the marital status of a woman, **Ms.**—e.g. **Dear Mr. Toler, Dear Miss Cameron, Dear Mrs. Nakamura, Dear Ms. Ingrao**. Women who feel that marital status should be no more specified in their own case than in that of a man (for whom **Mr.** serves, irrespective of whether he is married) prefer **Ms.** to **Mrs.** and **Miss.** The plural of **Mr.** is **Messrs.**; the plural of **Mrs.** or **Ms.** is **Mmes.**; the plural of **Miss** is **Misses**. Professional

Forms for Letters

titles may also be used in the salutation: **Dear Professor Newman, Dear Dr. Marton**. (*Webster's New Collegiate Dictionary* carries an extensive list of the forms of address for various dignitaries [judges, clergy, legislators, etc.].)

(f)   The body of the letter should be single-spaced, except for double-spacing between paragraphs. Paragraphs are not indented but start flush with the left-hand margin.

(g)   The usual complimentary closes for business letters are these: **Sincerely yours, Yours truly, Very truly yours**. The complimentary close is followed by a comma.

(h)   The writer should type his or her name about three or four spaces below the complimentary close. The typed name should not be prefaced with a professional title (e.g. **Dr., Rev.**) nor followed with a designation of academic degrees (e.g. **M.A., Ph.D.**), but below the typed name, the writer may indicate his or her official capacity (e.g. **President, Director of Personnel, Managing Editor**). The writer should sign his or her name in the space between the complimentary close and the typed name.

(i)   If one or more copies of the letter are being sent to others, that fact should be indicated with a notation like the following in the lower left-hand side of the page (**cc.** is the abbreviation of **carbon copy**):

   cc: Mary Hunter
      Robert Allison

(j)   If the letter was dictated to, and typed by, a secretary, that fact should be indicated by a notation like the following, which is typed flush with the left-hand margin and below the writer's signature (the writer's initials are given in capital letters, the secretary's in lowercase: **WLT/cs** or **WLT:cs**.

See the following models for the text and envelope of the two styles of business letters.

Format of Business Letter

SEMIBLOCK

239 Riverside Road
Columbus, OH 43210
January 5, 1981

Mr. Thomas J. Weiss
Manager, Survey Division
Acme Engineering Company, Inc.
5868 Fanshawe Drive
Omaha, NB 68131

Dear Mr. Weiss:

Mr. Robert Miller, sales representative of the Rushmore Caterpillar Company of Columbus and a long-time friend of my father, told me that when he saw you at a convention in Chicago recently, you indicated you would have two or three temporary positions open this summer in your division. Mr. Miller kindly offered to write you about me, but he urged me to write also.

By June, I will have completed my junior year in the Department of Civil Engineering at Ohio State University. Not only do I need to work this summer to finance my final year of college, but I also need to get some practical experience in surveying tracts on a large road-building project such as your company is now engaged in. After checking with several of the highway contractors in this area, I have learned that all of them have already hired their quota of engineering students for next summer.

For the last three summers, I have worked for the Worley Building Contractors of Columbus as a carpenter's helper and as a cement-finisher. Mr. Albert Michaels, my foreman for the last three summers, has indicated that he would write a letter of reference for me, if you want one. He understands why I want to get some experience in surveying this summer, but he told me that I would have priority for a summertime job with Worley if I wanted it.

Among my instructors in civil engineering, the two men who know me best are Dr. Theodore Sloan, who says that he knows you, and Mr. A. M. Slater. Currently, I have a 3.2 quality-point average in all my subjects, but I have straight A's in all my engineering courses. For the last two quarters, I have worked as a laboratory assistant for Professor Sloan.

I am anxious to get experience in my future profession, and I am quite willing to establish temporary residence in Omaha during the summer. I own a four-cylinder sub-compact car that I could use to travel to the job site each day. I am in good health, and I would be available to work for long hours and at odd hours during the summer months. If you want any letters of recommendation from any of the men named in my letter, please let me know.

Sincerely yours,

Oscar Jerman

cc. Robert Miller

BUSINESS LETTER TYPED ON PLAIN, UNLINED PAPER

ADDRESSED BUSINESS-SIZE ENVELOPE

Oscar Jerman
239 Riverside Road
Columbus, OH 43210

Mr. Thomas J. Weiss
Manager, Survey Division
Acme Engineering Company, Inc.
5868 Fanshawe Drive
Omaha, NB 68131

Format of Business Letter
FULL BLOCK

605 Third Avenue
New York, NY 10016
212-867-9800
Telex 12-7063
Cable JONWILE
*New York, Chichester,
Brisbane, Toronto*

John Wiley & Sons, Inc. Publishers

Educational Group

January 5, 1981

Ms. Jane Cordell
The Hammond Architectural Group
126 West Street
Van Nuys, CA 91401

Dear Ms. Cordell:

Thank you for your kind words about the writing texts you have purchased for the firm's reference library. We find more and more companies are setting up such libraries as they recognize that more information creates the need for more effective writing and general communication. I am glad that our texts have helped, and I am enclosing more information about our English list.

Your recent recruiting program for local college students apparently was a success. You mention your advising them that ideas which cannot be systematically communicated to colleagues are worthless ideas, and that your company recognizes the expanded role of college writing programs in the education of career-oriented students. I congratulate you on your acceptance of the inevitable, and I am sure that your advice does not fall on deaf ears. Most professionals who write to me know that good writing can define and therefore help solve a problem, and many students seem to be increasingly aware of this as well.

The new order for texts that you enclosed with your letter has been passed to our Distribution Department; allow three weeks for delivery. Please let me know if I can be of any other help, and thank you for your insightful letter.

Sincerely,

Clifford W. Mills

Clifford W. Mills
English Editor

CWM/ps
F/13

Enclosure

cc: Ms. Joan Howard

BUSINESS LETTER ON LETTERHEAD STATIONERY

LETTERHEAD BUSINESS ENVELOPE

Clifford W. Mills

John Wiley & Sons, Inc. Publishers
605 Third Avenue, New York, NY 10016

Ms. Jane Cordell
The Hammond Architectural Group
126 West Street
Van Nuys, CA 91401

The Two-Letter Postal Abbreviations

Here is the U.S. Postal Service list of two-letter abbreviations of the fifty states, the District of Columbia, and outlying areas. These abbreviations should be set down in capital letters without a period and should be followed by the appropriate five-digit ZIP code—for example, Tempe, AZ 85281.

Forms for Letters

Alabama	**AL**	Montana	**MT**
Alaska	**AK**	Nebraska	**NB**
Arizona	**AZ**	Nevada	**NV**
Arkansas	**AR**	New Hampshire	**NH**
California	**CA**	New Jersey	**NJ**
Colorado	**CO**	New Mexico	**NM**
Connecticut	**CT**	New York	**NY**
Delaware	**DE**	North Carolina	**NC**
District of Columbia	**DC**	North Dakota	**ND**
Florida	**FL**	Ohio	**OH**
Georgia	**GA**	Oklahoma	**OK**
Guam	**GU**	Oregon	**OR**
Hawaii	**HI**	Pennsylvania	**PA**
Idaho	**ID**	Puerto Rico	**PR**
Illinois	**IL**	Rhode Island	**RI**
Indiana	**IN**	South Carolina	**SC**
Iowa	**IA**	South Dakota	**SD**
Kansas	**KS**	Tennessee	**TN**
Kentucky	**KY**	Texas	**TX**
Louisiana	**LA**	Utah	**UT**
Maine	**ME**	Vermont	**VT**
Maryland	**MD**	Virgin Islands	**VI**
Massachusetts	**MA**	Virginia	**VA**
Michigan	**MI**	Washington	**WA**
Minnesota	**MN**	West Virginia	**WV**
Mississippi	**MS**	Wisconsin	**WI**
Missouri	**MO**	Wyoming	**WY**

A Résumé

A résumé (pronounced *rez-oo-may*) is a one- or two-page summary, presented in the form of a list, of a job-applicant's life, relevant personal experiences, education, work experience, extracurricular activities, honors, goals, etc. It is usually submitted, along with such documents as academic transcripts, letters of reference, and specimens of one's writing, as part of a formal application for a job. The résumé is also referred to, and sometimes even labeled with, the Latin phrases *curriculum vitae* (the course of one's life) or *vita brevis* (a short life) or simply *vita*.

Under the headings of Education, Work Experience, and Extracurricular Activities, items are usually listed in a reverse chronological order, starting with the most recent and ending with the earliest. (See the sample résumé.)

A dossier (mentioned in the sample résumé) is a collection of one's documents (transcripts, letters of reference, etc.), which is kept on file in a school's placement office and which will be mailed out, upon request, to prospective employers. The letters of reference in a dossier, written by teachers, employers, and acquaintances, are usually confidential—that is, they are never seen by the applicant. (According to a federal law passed in 1975, however, applicants must be allowed to see any letters of reference about themselves if the letters were written after the law was passed and if the applicants have not signed a waiver to see the letters.) The names and addresses of other people who have agreed to write letters of reference upon request are often listed in the résumé as Additional References.

A Résumé

Depending upon the kind of job being applied for, some of the other categories that could be included in a résumé are Travel, Languages, Community Service, Research, Publications, Teaching Experience.

Résumé

Mary Watson Evans
239 E. Torrence Rd.
Columbus, OH 43214
Tel: (614) 267-4819 (home)
(614) 422-6866 (office)

PERSONAL: Born, Milwaukee, Wisconsin, August 5, 1958

MARITAL STATUS: Married, James Evans, 1981; no children

EDUCATION: 1980-82, MBA (expected in June, 1982), Ohio State University, Columbus, OH
Major--Accounting
1976-80, BA, Marquette University, Milwaukee, WI, graduated magna cum laude, 1980
Major--Economics
Minor--History
1972-76, Westside High School, Milwaukee, WI, graduated summa cum laude, 1976

WORK EXPERIENCE: Research assistant for Robert Moberly, Professor of Finance,
Ohio State University, 1980-82
Check-out clerk, weekends and summers, A&P grocery store,
Milwaukee, WI, 1979-80
Clerk-typist, summer of 1976, Allis Chalmers of Milwaukee
Clerk, Saturdays and summers, Gimbel's Department Store,
Milwaukee, WI, 1974-75

EXTRA-CURRICULAR ACTIVITIES: Yearbook assistant editor, Marquette University, 1980
Freshman representative on Student Council, Marquette
University, 1976-77
Reporter, Westside High School newspaper, 1974;
editorial writer, 1975; editor, 1976

HONORS: $500 Scholarship from Rush Foundation, 1976-77
Full-tuition Scholarship from Omicron Society, 1979-80
Quill and Scroll award for Best Reporting, 1974

CAREER GOALS: Position as accountant or editor of in-house journal in a large
accounting firm or bank in the Chicago area, where my husband,
who will take his law degree in June, 1982, has accepted a position.
I plan to take night courses in commercial law.

REFERENCES: My dossier is on file at the Placement Office, Ohio State University,
164 W. 17th Avenue, Columbus, OH 43210

Additional letters of reference (besides those in my dossier):

Mr. John Anderson
Personnel Manager
Allis Chalmers Corporation
West Allis, WI 53214

Mr. Hans Schmitz
Manager, A&P Stores (retired)
2841 N. 70th Street
Milwaukee, WI 53210

Glossary of Usage

Many of the entries here deal with pairs of words that writers often confuse because the words look alike or sound alike. Ascertain the distinctions between these confusing pairs and then invent your own memorizing devices to help you make the right choice in a particular case. In all cases of disputed usage, the most conservative position on that usage is presented so that you can decide whether you can afford to run the risk of alienating that segment of your readers who subscribe to the conservative position.

affect, effect.   The noun form is almost always **effect** (*The effect of that usage was to alienate the purists*). The wrong choices are usually made when writers use the verb. The verb **effect** means "to bring about," "to accomplish" (*The prisoner effected his escape by picking a lock*). The verb **affect** means "to influence" (*The weather affected her moods*).

allusion, illusion.   Think of **allusion** as meaning "indirect reference" (*He made an allusion to her parents*). Think of **illusion** as meaning "a deceptive impression" (*He continued to entertain this illusion about her ancestry*).

Glossary of Usage

alot, a lot. This locution should always be written as two words (*A lot of the natives lost faith in the government*).

alright, allright, all right. **All right** is the only correct way to write this expression (*He told his mother that he was all right*).

altogether, all together. **Altogether** is the adverb form in the sense of "completely" (*She was not altogether happy with the present*). **All together** is the adjective form in the sense of "collectively" (*The students were all together in their loyalty to the team*).

among. See **between**.

amount of, number of. When you are speaking of masses or bulks, use **amount of** (*They bought a large amount of sugar*). When you are speaking of persons or things that can be counted one by one, use **number of** (*They bought a large number of cookies*). See **fewer, less**.

as, like. See **like**

because of. See **due to**

beside, besides. Both of these words are used as prepositions, but **beside** means "at the side of" (*They built a cabin beside a lake*), and **besides** means "in addition to" (*They bought a jacket besides a pair of boots*).

between. The conservative position is that between should be used only when two persons or things are involved (*They made a choice between the Democrat and the Republican*).

can't help but. Conservatives regard this expression as an instance of a double negative (**can't** and **but**). They would re-write the sentence *She can't help but love him* as *She can't help loving him*.

center around. One frequently sees and hears this expression (e.g. *His interest centered around his work*). The expression seems to violate the basic metaphor from which it derives. How can something center **around** something else? Say instead *"His interest centered on his work"* or *"His interest centered upon his work."*

continual, continuous. There is a real distinction between these two adjectives. Think of **continual** as referring to something that occurs repeatedly (i.e. with interruptions). For instance, a noise that occurred every three or four minutes would be a "continual noise"; a noise that persisted without interruption for an hour would be a "continuous noise." **Continual** is stop-and-go; **continuous** is an uninterrupted flow.

could of, should of, would of. In the spoken language, these forms sound very much like the correct written forms. In writing, use the correct forms **could have, should have, would have** or, in informal contexts, the contractions **could've, should've, would've**.

data. The word **data**, like the words **criteria** and **phenomena**, is a plural noun and therefore demands the plural form of the demonstrative adjective (*these data, those data*) and the plural form of the verb (*These data present convincing evidence of his guilt. The data were submitted by the committee*).

different from, different than. In British usage, **different than** is more likely to be used than **different from** when a clause follows the expression (e.g. *This treatment is different than we expected*). In conservative American usage, **different from** is preferred to **different than**, whether the expression is followed with a noun phrase (*The British usage is different from the American usage*) or with a noun clause (*This treatment is different from what we expected*).

disinterested, uninterested. Careful writers still make a distinction between these two words. For them, **disinterested**

Glossary of Usage

means "unbiased," "impartial," "objective" (*The mother could not make a disinterested judgment about her son*). **Uninterested**, for them, means "bored," "indifferent to" (*The students were obviously uninterested in the lecture*).

due to, because of. Many writers use **due to** and **because of** interchangeably. Some writers, however, observe the conservative distinction between these two expressions: **due to** is an adjectival construction, and **because of** is an adverbial construction. Accordingly, they would always follow any form of the verb **to be** (**is, were, has been,** etc.) with **due to** (*Due to illness, he was absent all week*), and they would always follow transitive and intransitive verbs with the adverbial construction **because of** (*She missed the party because of illness. He failed because of illness*). Sometimes, they substitute **owing to** or **on account of** for **because of**.

effect. See **affect**.

fewer, less. Use **fewer** with countable items (*Louise has fewer hats than Emily does*). Use **less** when speaking of mass or bulk (*Elmer has less sand in his garden than Andrew does*). See **amount of, number of**.

human, humans. Those who take a conservative view of language have not yet accepted **human** or **humans** as a noun. They would rewrite "The natives made no distinction between animals and humans" as "The natives made no distinction between animals and human beings." In their view, **human** should be used only as an adjective.

imply, infer. There is a definite difference in meaning between these two verbs. **Imply** means "to hint at," "to suggest" (*She implied that she wouldn't come to his party*). **Infer** means "to deduce," "to draw a conclusion from" (*He inferred from the look on her face that she wouldn't come to his party*).

kind of, sort of.   Do not use the article **a** or **an** with either of these phrases (*He suffered some kind of a heart attack. She got the sort of an ovation she deserved*). **Kind of** and **sort of** in the sense of "rather" or "somewhat" (*He was kind of annoyed with his teacher*) should be reserved for an informal or a colloquial context.

lend, loan.   The conservative position is that **loan** should be used exclusively as a noun (*He took out a loan from the bank*) and that **lend** should be used exclusively as a verb (*The bank lends him the downpayment*).

less.   See **fewer**.

lie, lay.   **Lie** (past tense **lay**, past participle **lain**) is an intransitive verb meaning "to rest," "to recline" (*The book lies on the table. It has lain there for three days*). **Lay** (past tense **laid**, past participle **laid**) is a transitive verb (i.e. must be followed by an object) meaning "to put down" (*She lays the book on the table. Yesterday she laid the book on the mantelpiece*).

like, as.   Avoid the use of **like** as a subordinating conjunction (*At a party, he behaves like he does in church*). Use **like** exclusively as a preposition (*At a party, he behaves like a prude*). **As** is the appropriate subordinating conjunction with clauses (*At a party, he behaves as he does in church*).

literally.   Originally, **literally** was used as an adverb meaning the opposite of **figuratively**. In recent years, some people have been using the word as an intensifier (*She literally blew her top*). Careful writers still use the word in its original sense of "actually" (*The mother literally washed out her son's mouth with soap*).

loose, lose.   These words look alike but do not sound alike. Here is a device to help you remember the difference in meaning. The two *o*'s in **loose** are like two marbles dumped

Glossary of Usage

out of a can (*The dog broke its leash and ran loose in the backyard*). The word **lose** has lost one of its *o*'s (*I always lose my wallet when I go to a carnival*). If these memorizing devices do not help you keep the two words straight, invent your own device.

past, passed.   These words are more sound-alikes than look-alikes. The word with the *-ed* is the only one that can be used as a verb (*His car passed mine on the freeway*). The word **past** is versatile: it can be used as a noun (*I recalled my sordid past*), as an adjective (*I recalled the past events*), and as a preposition (*His car sped past mine like a bullet*), but it is never used as a verb.

principal, principle.   These words sound alike, but they are spelled differently, and they have different meanings. Whether used as a noun or as an adjective, **principal** carries the meaning of "chief." The chief of a high school is the **principal**. The adjective that means "chief" is always *principal* (*The principal is the principal administrative officer of a high school*). The word **principle** is used only as a noun and means "rule," "law" (*A manufacturer shouldn't ignore the basic principles of physics*).

quote(s).   In formal contexts, use **quotation(s)** instead of the colloquial contraction **quote(s)**.

reason is because.   This phrasing constitutes an example of faulty predication (see section **40**). Write "the reason is that . . ."

reason why.   This phrasing is redundant. Instead of writing "The reason why I am unhappy is that I lost my wallet," drop the redundant **why** and write "The reason I am unhappy is that I lost my wallet."

respectfully, respectively.   Choose the correct adverb for what you want to say. **Respectfully** means "with respect"

(*She answered her mother respectfully*). **Respectively** means "the previously mentioned items in the order in which they are listed" (*Mary Sarton, Emily Doan, and Sarah Fowler were the first, second, and third presidents of the Guild, respectively*).

should of.   See **could of**.

so, such.   Avoid the use of **so** or **such** as an unqualified intensifier, as in sentences like "She was so happy," "It was such a cold day." If you must use an intensifier, use such adverbs as **very, exceedingly, unusually** (*She was very happy. It was an unusually cold day*). If you use **so** or **such** to modify an adjective, your readers have a right to expect you to complete the structure with a *that*-clause of result (*She was so happy that she clapped her hands for joy. It was so cold that we clapped our hands to keep warm*).

sort of.   See **kind of**.

supposed to, used to.   Because it is difficult to hear the *-d* when these phrases are spoken, writers sometimes write "He was suppose to come yesterday. He use to come at noon." Always add the *-d* to these words.

their, there, they're.   All three words are pronounced alike. The wrong one is chosen in a particular instance, not because the writer does not know better but because the writer has been careless or inattentive. There [their? they're?] is no need to review the different meanings of these very common words.

try and.   In the spoken medium, one frequently hears utterances like "Try and stay within the white lines if you can." Purists still insist that we write "Try to stay within the white lines if you can." So if we want to be "proper," we should always write **try to** instead of **try and**.

used to.   See **supposed to**.

Glossary of Usage

whose, who's.   Since the two words are pronounced alike, it is understandable that writers sometimes make the wrong choice. The word spelled with the apostrophe is the contraction of "who is" (*Who's the principal actor? Who's playing the lead role?*) **Whose** is (1) the interrogative pronoun (*Whose hat is this?*), (2) the possessive case of the relative pronoun **who** (*John is the man whose son died last week*), (3) an acceptable possessive form of the relative pronoun **which** (*Our flag, whose broad stripes and bright stars we watched through the perilous fight, was gallantly streaming over the ramparts*).

would of.   See **could of**.

Glossary of Grammatical Terms

Some of these terms are defined in the sections where they figure prominently. But since many of these terms also occur in sections where they are not defined, this glossary is provided for the convenience of the curious but puzzled reader.

active verb.   See **passive verb.**

adjective clause.   An adjective clause is a dependent clause that modifies a noun or a pronoun, much as a simple adjective does.

The relative pronouns **who, which,** and **that** often appear at the head of the adjective clause, serving as the connecting link between the modified noun or pronoun and the clause, which then follows.

The car, **which was old and battered,** served us well.

Those are the houses **that I love best.**

Sometimes the relative pronoun is unexpressed but understood:

The book **I was reading** held my attention. (Here **that** is understood: The book **that** I was reading.)

See **dependent clause, relative pronoun, restrictive**

Glossary of Grammatical Terms

adjective clause, nonrestrictive adjective clause, modifier.

adverb clause. An adverb clause is a dependent clause that modifies a verb or verbal, much as a simple adverb does.

The subordinating conjunction (**when, because, so that,** etc.), which appears at the head of the clause, links the adverb clause to the word that it modifies.

When I was ready, I took the examination.

I took the examination **because I was ready.**

To take an examination **when you are not ready** is dangerous.

(Here the adverb clause modifies the infinitive **to take.**)

See **dependent clause, subordinating conjunction, verbal, modifier.**

antecedent. An antecedent is the noun that a pronoun refers to or "stands for."

In the previous sentence, for example, the antecedent of the relative pronoun **that** is **noun.** In the sentence "The mother told her son that his check had arrived," **mother** is the antecedent of the pronoun **her,** and **son** is the antecedent of the pronoun **his.**

See **relative pronoun.**

auxiliary verbs. Auxiliary verbs are those function words— "helping" words (hence, *auxiliary*)—that accompany other verb forms to indicate tense or mood or voice.

The following words in boldface are auxiliary verbs:

She **will** walk to work. She **is** walking to work. She **has** walked to work.

She **has been** walking to work. She **could** walk to work. She **must** walk to work.

She **was** driven to work.

See **voice.**

comma splice. A comma splice is the use of a comma, instead of a coordinating conjunction or a semicolon, between the two independent clauses of a compound sentence.

> He could not tolerate noise, noise made him nervous and irritable.

Since the comma is a separating device rather than a joining device, it must be accompanied in this sentence by a coordinating conjunction (here **for**), or it must be replaced with a semicolon.

See **independent clause, compound sentence, coordinating conjunction.**

complement.   A complement is the word or phrase, following a verb, that "completes" the predicate of a clause.

A complement may be (1) the object of a transitive verb (He hit **the ball**), (2) the noun or noun phrase following the verb **to be** (He is **an honors student**), or (3) the adjective following the verb **to be** or a linking verb (He is **happy**. The milk tastes **sour**.).

See **transitive verb, linking verb, to be, predicate complement, noun phrase.**

complex sentence.   A complex sentence is one that consists of one independent clause and one or more dependent clauses.

The following complex sentence has two dependent clauses —the first one an adverb clause, the second an adjective clause:

> **When she got to the microphone,** she made a proposal **that won unanimous approval.**

As used by grammarians, the term has nothing to do with the length or complexity of the sentence.

See **independent clause, dependent clause.**

compound sentence.   A compound sentence is one that consists of two or more independent clauses.

> He was twenty-one, but she was only eighteen.
> Young men are idealists; old men are realists.

Glossary of Grammatical Terms

See **independent clause, comma splice.**

coordinate. Words, phrases, and clauses of the same grammatical kind or of equal rank are said to be "coordinate."

A pair or series of nouns, for instance, would be a coordinate unit. An infinitive phrase yoked with a participial phrase would not be a coordinate unit, because the phrases are not of the same grammatical kind. An independent clause would not be coordinate with a dependent or subordinate clause, because the two clauses are not of equal rank. An alternative term for **coordinate** is **parallel.**

See **parallelism, coordinating conjunction.**

coordinating conjunction. A coordinating conjunction is a word that joins words, phrases, or clauses of the same kind or rank. It joins nouns with nouns, verbs with verbs, prepositional phrases with prepositional phrases, independent clauses with independent clauses, adverb clauses with adverb clauses, etc.

A coordinating conjunction cannot be used to join a noun with an adjective, a prepositional phrase with a gerund phrase, or an independent clause with a dependent clause.

The coordinating conjunctions are **and, but, or, for, nor, yet, so.**

See **coordinate, correlative conjunctions, subordinating conjunction.**

correlative conjunctions. Correlative conjunctions are coordinating conjunctions that operate in pairs to join coordinate structures in a sentence.

The common correlative conjunctions are **either . . . or, neither . . . nor, both . . . and, not only . . . but also,** and **whether . . . or.**

By this act, she renounced **both** her citizenship **and** her civil rights.

faulty predication

See **coordinate, coordinating conjunction.**

dangling verbal   A dangling verbal is a participle, gerund, or infinitive (or a phrase formed with one of these verbals) that is either unattached to a noun or pronoun or attached to the wrong noun or pronoun.

> Raising his glass, a toast was proposed to the newlyweds by the bride's father.

In this sentence, the participial phrase **raising his glass** is attached to the wrong noun **(toast)** and therefore is said to be "dangling" (it was not the **toast** that was doing the **raising**). The participial phrase will be properly attached if the noun **father** is made the subject of the sentence:

See **verbal** and **verbal phrase.**

dependent clause.   A dependent clause is a group of words that has a subject and a finite verb but that is made part of, or dependent on, a larger structure by a relative pronoun **(who, which, that)** or by a subordinating conjunction (**when, if, because, although,** etc.).

There are three kinds of dependent clause: adjective clause, adverb clause, and noun clause.

A dependent clause cannot stand by itself; it must be joined to an independent clause to make it part of a complete sentence. A dependent clause written with an initial capital letter and with a period or question mark at the end of it is one of the structures that are called *sentence fragments*. An alternative term is **subordinate clause.**

See **independent clause, finite verb, adjective clause, adverb clause, noun clause, subordinating conjunction.**

faulty predication.   A faulty predication occurs when the verb or verb phrase of a clause does not fit semantically or syntactically with the subject or noun phrase of the clause. It results from the choice of incompatible words or structures.

Glossary of Grammatical Terms

The shortage of funds **claimed** more money.

The reason I couldn't go **was because I hadn't completed my homework.**

The verb **claimed** in the first sentence is semantically incompatible with the noun phrase **the shortage of funds** that serves as the subject of the clause. In the second sentence, the adverbial **because** clause is syntactically incompatible as a predicate complement following the verb **was.**

See **predicate complement, predicate verb, noun phrase, verb phrase.**

finite verb.   A finite verb is a verb that is fixed or limited, by its form, in person, number, and tense.

In the sentence "The boy runs to school," the verb **runs** is fixed by its form in person (cf. **I run, you run**), in number (cf. **they run**), and in tense (cf. **he ran**). The verbals (participle, gerund, infinitive) are considered **infinite verbs** because although they are fixed by their form in regard to tense (present or past), they are not limited in person or number. The minimal units of a clause, whether it is dependent or independent, are a subject (a noun phrase) and a finite verb:

Bells ring. (but not: Bells ringing)

See **predicate verb, noun phrase, verbals.**

fused sentence.   A fused sentence is the joining of two or more independent clauses without any punctuation or coordinating conjunction between them.

She could not believe her eyes mangled bodies were strewn all over the highway.

A fused sentence is also called a **run-on sentence** or a **run-together sentence.**

See **independent clause, comma splice.**

gerund.   A gerund is a word that is formed from a verb but that functions as a noun.

Because of its hybrid nature as part verb and part noun, a gerund may take an object, may be modified by an adverb, and may serve in the sentence in any function in which a noun can perform. Since, like the present participle, it is formed by adding **-ing** to the base verb, one can distinguish the gerund from the participle by noting whether it functions in the sentence as a noun rather than as an adjective. The following are examples of the gerund or gerund phrase performing various functions of the noun:

As subject of the sentence: **Hiking** is his favorite exercise.

As object of a verb: He favored **raising the funds by subscription.**

As complement of the verb **to be:** His most difficult task was **reading all the fine print.**

As object of preposition: After **reading the book,** he took the examination.

The latter sentence would be considered a dangling verbal if it were phrased as follows: After reading the book, the examination had to be taken.

See **verbal phrase, dangling verbal.**

independent clause.   An independent clause is a group of words that has a subject and a finite verb and that is not made part of a larger structure by a relative pronoun or a subordinating conjunction.

The following group of words is an independent clause because it has a subject and a finite verb:

The **girls tossed** the ball.

The following group of words has the same subject and finite verb, but it is not an independent clause because it is made part of a larger structure by the subordinating conjunction **when:**

When the girls tossed the ball.

Glossary of Grammatical Terms

The **when** turns the clause into an adverb clause and thereby makes it part of a larger structure—a sentence consisting of a dependent clause (the adverb clause) and an independent clause (which must be supplied here to make a complete sentence).

See **dependent clause, finite verb, subordinating conjunction, relative pronoun.**

infinitive.   An infinitive is a word that is formed from a verb but that functions in the sentence as a noun or as an adjective or as an adverb.

Capable of functioning in these ways, the infinitive is more versatile than the participle, which functions only as an adjective, or the gerund, which functions only as a noun. The infinitive is formed by putting **to** in front of the base form of the verb.

Here are some examples of the infinitive or infinitive phrase in its various functions:

As noun (subject of sentence): **To err** is human; **to forgive** is divine.

As adjective (modifying a noun—in this case, **place**): He wanted a place **to store his furniture.**

As adverb (modifying a verb—in this case, **waved**): He waved a handkerchief **to gain her attention.**

The infinitive phrase in the following sentence would be considered a dangling verbal:

To prevent infection, the finger should be thoroughly washed.
(Corrected: To prevent infection, you should wash the finger thoroughly.)

See **verbal phrase, dangling verbal.**

intransitive verb.   An intransitive verb is a verb that expresses action but that does not take an object.

Intransitive verbs cannot be turned into the passive voice. Most action verbs in English have both transitive and intransitive uses, like **I ran swiftly** (intransitive) and **I ran the streetcar** (transitive). But some verbs can be used only transitively, like the verb *to emit*, and some verbs can be used only intransitively, like the verb *to go*. If in doubt about whether a particular verb can be used both transitively and intransitively, consult a dictionary.

The following verbs are all used intransitively:

He **swam** effortlessly.

They **slept** for twelve hours.

She **quarreled** with her neighbors.

See **transitive verb, passive verb, voice.**

linking verb. Linking verbs are those verbs of the senses like **feel, look, smell, taste, sound,** and a limited number of other verbs like **seem, remain, become, appear,** that "link" the subject of the sentence with a complement.

Linking verbs are followed by an adjective or a noun or a noun phrase:

The sweater **felt** soft. (adjective as complement)

He **appeared** calm. (adjective as complement)

She **remains** the president of the union.(noun phrase as complement)

See **to be, complement, predicate complement, noun phrase.**

modifier. A modifier is a word, phrase, or clause that limits, specifies, qualifies, or describes another word.

In the phrase "the red barn," the adjectival modifier **red** helps to specify or describe the particular barn being talked about. In the phrase "ran swiftly," the adverbial modifier **swiftly** describes the manner in which the action designated in the verb **ran** was done. Phrases and clauses also modify nouns and verbs:

the girl **with the flowery hat** (prepositional phrase modifying **girl**)

the barn **that is painted red** (adjective clause modifying **barn**)

he ran **down the street** (prepositional phrase modifying **ran**)

Glossary of Grammatical Terms

he ran **because he was frightened** (adverb clause modifying **ran**)

Besides modifying verbs, adverbs also modify adjectives and other adverbs:

It was an **unusually** brilliant color. (modifying the adjective **brilliant**)

He ran **very** swiftly. (modifying the adverb **swiftly**)

See **adjective clause, adverb clause.**

nonrestrictive adjective clause. A nonrestrictive adjective clause is an adjective clause that supplies information about the noun or pronoun that it modifies but information that is not needed to identify or specify the particular noun or pronoun being talked about.

My father, **who is a college graduate,** cannot get a job.

In this sentence, the adjective clause **who is a college graduate** supplies information about the father, but that information is not needed to identify which father is being talked about. The particular father being talked about is sufficiently identified by the **my.**

A nonrestrictive adjective clause must be separated with a comma from the noun or pronoun that it modifies.

See **adjective clause, restrictive adjective clause, modifier.**

noun clause. A noun clause is a dependent clause that can serve almost every function that a noun or pronoun or noun phrase can serve: as subject of the sentence, as an appositive to a noun, as the complement of a verb, as object of a preposition, but not as an indirect object.

The subordinating conjunctions that most often introduce a noun clause are **that** and **whether**—although **that** is sometimes omitted when the noun clause serves as the object of a transitive verb.

That she would make the grade was evident to everyone. (subject of sentence)

He said **he would not come.** (object of verb; **that** is omitted here, but it is just as correct to say **that he would come**)

The fact **that I had been sick** did not influence their decision. (in apposition to **fact**)

They asked me about **whether I had seen him recently.** (object of the preposition **about**)

See **dependent clause, noun phrase, complement.**

noun phrase. A noun phrase consists of a noun or a pronoun and all of its modifiers (if any).

In the following sentence all of the words in boldface would be considered part of the noun phrase, which is dominated by the noun **house**:

The big, rambling, clapboard house on the hill belongs to Mrs. Adams.

See **verb phrase, verbal phrase.**

parallelism. Parallelism is the grammatical principle that words, phrases, or clauses joined in a pair or in a series must be of the same kind.

Nouns must be coupled with nouns; prepositional phrases must be coupled with prepositional phrases; adjective clauses must be coupled with adjective clauses.

Parallelism breaks down, for instance, when a noun is yoked with an adjective or a prepositional phrase is yoked with a participial phrase. Parallelism has been preserved in the following sentence, because all the words in the series that serves as the predicate complement of the verb **was** are adjectives:

The engine was **compact, durable,** and **efficient.**

See **coordinate, coordinating conjunction.**

participle. A participle is a word that is formed from a verb but that functions as an adjective.

Because of its hybrid nature as part verb and part adjective, a participle may take an object, may be modified by an adverb, and may modify a noun or a pronoun.

Glossary of Grammatical Terms

> Pulling his gun quickly from his holster, the sheriff fired a shot be-
> fore the burglar could jump him.

In that sentence, the participle **pulling** takes an object **(gun)**, is modified by the adverb **quickly** and by the prepositional phrase **from his holster,** and modifies the noun **sheriff.**

The **present participle** is formed by adding **-ing** to the base form of the verb: **pulling, jumping, being.**

The **past participle** is formed by adding **-ed** or **-en** to the base form of the verb or by a special spelling: **pulled, beaten, left, bought.**

The **perfect participle** is formed with **having** plus the past participle form: **having pulled, having beaten, having left.**

The **passive participle** is formed with **having** plus **been** plus the past participle form: **having been pulled, having been beaten, having been left.**

See **verbal phrase, dangling verbal.**

passive verb.   A passive verb is the form that a predicate verb takes when we want to indicate that the subject of the sentence is the receiver, not the doer, of the action.

The form that we use when we want to indicate that the subject is the doer of the action is called the **active verb.**

Only transitive verbs can be turned into the passive form. The passive verb is made by using some form of the verb **to be** (e.g. **am, is, are, was, were, has been**) and the past participle of the base verb.

> The shepherds **tend** the sheep. (active verb)
> The sheep **are tended** by the shepherds. (passive verb)

See **predicate verb, transitive verb, past participle, to be.**

predicate complement.   Some grammarians use the term **predicate complement** to refer to any noun, pronoun, or adjective that follows, or "completes," the verb, whether it be a transitive verb, a linking verb, or the verb **to be.** Other grammarians use the term **object** for the noun or pronoun that follows a transitive verb and reserve the term **predicate complement** for the noun, pronoun, or adjective that follows a linking verb or the verb **to be.**

She is the **president.** (noun following the verb **to be**)
She became the **breadwinner.** (noun following the linking verb)
The pie tastes **good.** (adjective following the linking verb)

See complement, transitive verb, linking verb, to be.

predicate verb. A predicate verb is the finite-verb part of the verb phrase that constitutes the whole predicate of a dependent or independent clause.

In the following sentence, the word in boldface is the predicate verb of the independent clause:

The man **guided** the dogsled through the blinding snowstorm.

See finite verb, verb phrase.

relative pronoun. The relative pronouns **who, which, that** serve a grammatical function in an adjective clause (as subject of the clause, as object or predicate complement of the verb of the clause, as object of a preposition in the clause) and also as the connecting link between the adjective clause and the noun or pronoun that the clause modifies.

Who is the only one of these relative pronouns that is inflected: **who** (nominative case), **whose** (possessive case), **whom** (objective case).

See dependent clause, adjective clause, antecedent.

restrictive adjective clause. A restrictive adjective clause is an adjective clause that identifies or specifies the noun or pronoun that it modifies, that "restricts" the meaning to a particular person, place, thing, or idea.

Baseball players who are under contract to a duly franchised professional team are eligible for a pension.

In this sentence, the adjective clause **who are under contract to . . . team** specifies those baseball players who are

Glossary of Grammatical Terms

eligible for a pension. If that adjective clause were enclosed with commas (that is, if it were a **nonrestrictive** clause), the sentence would mean that *all* baseball players are eligible *because* they are under contract to a professional team—a quite different meaning from the sentence that does not have commas enclosing the adjective clause.

A restrictive adjective clause should *not* be separated with a comma from the noun or pronoun that it modifies.

See **adjective clause, nonrestrictive clause, modifier.**

run-on sentence. See **fused sentence.**

semantics. Semantics is the branch of linguistics that deals with the study of the meanings of words. As explained in the headnote to the Grammar section of this handbook (pp. 9–13), in order to make sense of any language, we must know the meanings of individual words (semantics) and the grammar of that language.

sentence fragment. See **independent clause, dependent clause, finite verb.**

stem form. The·stem form of the verb is the form that combines with **to** to become the infinitive—**to walk, to go.** The stem form is also the same form that a verb has when it is used with the first-person pronouns in the present tense—**I walk, we go.**

See **tense.**

subordinating conjunction. A subordinating conjunction is a word that serves as the connecting link between an adverb clause or a noun clause and a word in some other structure.

The most common subordinating conjunctions that connect an adverb clause to the verb or verbal that the clause modifies are **when, whenever, because, since, although, though, while, as, after, before, unless, until, in order that, so that.**

The two subordinating conjunctions that serve as the link between the noun clause and another structure are **that** and **whether.** The conjunction **that** is often omitted when the noun clause functions as the object of a verb:

She said [that] the committee would not accept the proposal.

See **coordinating conjunction, adverb clause, noun clause.**

syntax. Syntax is the branch of grammar that deals with the study of how words are put together to form meaningful phrases or clauses in a particular language. Because modern English is not an inflected language like Latin, it depends mainly on word order to signal how groups of words are related to convey meaning. The phrase "the box big in" is not a meaningful unit in English; English syntax allows this arrangement of those words: "in the big box."

tense. Tense is that aspect of a verb which indicates the *time* of the action or state expressed in the verb. Here are the various tenses of the English verb, with an indication of how they are formed:

(1) **present tense**—formed with the stem form of the verb (**I run, you run**) or with **-s** added to the stem form in the third person singular (**she runs**) or with some form of the auxiliary verb **to be** and the present participle of the verb (**I am going, they are going**);

(2) **past tense**—formed by adding **-ed** to the stem form of the verb (**walk-ed, add-ed**) or by changing the spelling (**go, went; sing, sang; speak, spoke; is, was**) or with some form of the auxiliary verb **to be** and the present participle of the verb (**I was going, they were going**);

(3) **future tense**—formed with the auxiliary verb **shall** or **will** and the stem form of the verb (**you will go, we shall go**);

(4) **perfect tense**—formed with the auxiliary verb **has** or

Glossary of Grammatical Terms

have and the past participle of the verb (**I have walked, he has walked, they have walked**);

(5) **past-perfect tense**—formed with the auxiliary verb **had** and the past participle of the verb (**you had walked, we had walked**);

(6) **future-perfect tense**—formed with the auxiliary verbs **shall have** or **will have** and the past participle of the verb (**I shall have sung, she will have sung, they will have sung**).

See **auxiliary verbs, participle, stem form.**

to be.   **To be** is the infinitive form of the most frequently used verb in the English language, one that can be followed by a noun, a pronoun, an adjective, an adverb of place (e.g. **there, here, upstairs**), a preposition plus the object of the preposition (e.g. He is **like his father**), a verbal or verbal phrase, or a noun clause.

Here are the various forms of **to be,** as it changes in number, person, and tense: **am, is, are, was, were, shall be, will be, has been, have been, had been, shall have been, will have been.**

Some form of **to be** along with the present participle of the base verb is also used to form the progressive tense of the English verb: He **was going** to the doctor regularly. He **had been going** to the doctor regularly.

Some form of **to be** along with the past participle of the base verb is also used to form a passive verb: He **was struck** on the head. He **has been struck** on the head.

See **linking verb, predicate complement, passive verb, participle.**

transitive verb.   A transitive verb is a verb expressing action that terminates in, or is received by, an object.

The object of a transitive verb can be a noun or noun phrase, a pronoun, a verbal or verbal phrase, or a noun clause.

They **destroyed** the village. (noun as object)
They **shot** him. (pronoun as object)
She **favors** giving me another chance. (gerund phrase as object)
He **will try** to break the lock. (infinitive phrase as object)
She **proposed** that everyone in the room be allowed to vote.
(noun clause as object)

Only a transitive verb can be turned into a passive verb.

See **intransitive verb, passive verb.**

verb phrase.   A verb phrase is a group of words consisting of
a verb and all of its auxiliaries (if any), all of its complements
(if any), and all of its modifiers (if any).

In the following sentence, all words in boldface would be
considered part of the verb phrase (a structure dominated by
the verb):

The army **has been severely restricted in its operations.**

See **noun phrase, verbal phrase, predicate verb, auxiliary verb, modifier.**

verbal.   A verbal is the general name applied to participles,
gerunds, and infinitives.

These words are called verbals because they are formed
from verbs; because they are not finite verbs, they cannot by
themselves serve as the predicate verb of an independent
clause or a dependent clause.

See **participle, gerund, infinitive, finite verb, predicate
verb.**

verbal phrase.   A verbal phrase is a group of words consisting of a participle or a gerund or an infinitive and all of its
complements (if any) and all of its modifiers (if any).

In the following sentence, all words in boldface would be
considered part of the verbal phrase, which is dominated by
the participle **leaving:**

Leaving behind all of its heavy equipment, the army pressed
forward quickly.

voice.   Voice is that aspect of a verb which shows the relation of the subject to the action, i.e. whether that of performer or recipient. The former is called **active voice** (I loved her), the latter **passive voice** (I was loved).

See **passive verb.**

Commonly Misspelled Words

accept (cf. except)
accidentally
acquire
acquaintance
address
all right
already (cf. all ready)
arithmetic
athletics
attendance

believe
benign
business

cemetery
changeable
chief
choose (cf. chose)
conscience
correspondent

definite

dependent
design
devise (cf. device)
diminution
disappearance
dispel

effect (cf. affect)
embarrass
environment
exaggerate
existence

familiar
fascinate
flagrant
foreign
forth (cf. fourth)
fragrant
friend
fulfill *or* fulfil
    (but not *fullfill*)

Commonly Mispelled Words

government

harass
height
hindrance

incredible
independent
irresistible
its (cf. it's)

judgment

library
literature
lose (cf. loose)

maintenance (cf. maintain)
mathematics
minuscule
miracle
miscellaneous
mischief

necessary
neighbor
noticeable
nuisance

occasion
occurrence
occurred
offered
omitted

parallel

peculiar
possess
preceding (cf. proceeding)
prejudice
principal (cf. principle)
privilege

quite (cf. quiet)

receive
referring
relieve
remuneration
resemblance
reverence
ridiculous

seize
separate
similar
special
stationary (immobile)
stationery (paper)
succeed

than (cf. then)
their (cf. there)
threshold
too (cf. to)
tragedy
truly

usually

whose (cf. who's)
withhold

Index

Index

Index

Index